SELF-Parenting For LIFE:

LIVING A LIFETIME FROM THE SELF-PARENTING POINT-OF-VIEW

John K. Pollard, III

Disclaimer: The information and procedures contained in this book are based on the personal research and professional experience of the author. The publishers present the information in this book for educational purposes only. It is not intended as a substitute for consulting with your physician or mental health care provider. The author and publishers are not responsible for any adverse effects or consequences resulting from the use of any of the suggestions, preparations, or procedures discussed in this book. A health care professional should supervise all matters pertaining to your health.

Copyright © 2020 by John K. Pollard, III

All rights reserved. No part of this publication, text or illustrations, may be reproduced or transmitted in any form or by any means without express written permission of the publisher.

Published by:

Generic Human Studies Publishing
8019 Jefferson St, Paramount,
CA, 90723 USA
Phone: 562-633-1259

ISBN 0-942055-02-3

Dedication

As per always, any SELF-Parenting book I write
is dedicated to the Living Memory of
Max Freedom Long,
without who's life and dedication
SELF-Parenting would not be with us today.

Acknowledgments

Many wonderful SELF-Parenting Practitioners have
contributed to the creation of this book. Specifically, I would
like to thank Christine Armstrong for ongoing support
and contributions.

Foreword

Dear Reader,

The purpose of this book is to provide the daily practitioner of SELF-Parenting a lifetime overview to guide his/her long-term growth into the deeper levels of SELF-Parenting awareness. In practical terms, the ideal reader would have been practicing the SPP for five years or more.

If, by chance, this is your first introduction to the concept of SELF-Parenting you are best served by setting it aside and beginning your exploration with *SELF-Parenting: The Complete Guide to Your Inner Conversations*. Often called the "yellow book," this is where the introductory concepts and practical steps of SELF-Parenting are described.

These pages are meant to be an ongoing guide for the Intermediate to Advanced Practitioner of the SELF-Parenting Program. It's designed to guide your daily practice of SELF-Parenting over approximately a 30-year period. As such, it does not explain any of the introductory practices upon which this work is based.

Once you have practiced SELF-Parenting daily for 6 months to 2 years, there is a second book called *The SELF-Parenting Program, Core Guidelines for the SELF-Parenting Practitioner*, also known as the "blue book." This book provides essential guidelines for this level of practitioner.

Essentially both these books, along with many years of ongoing daily SELF-Parenting sessions are prerequisites for you to fully apply the material presented in the following pages.

That being said, I have done my best to provide an enjoyable reading experience even for a non-practitioner of SELF-Parenting in the hopes he/she will be further inspired to begin daily SELF-Parenting sessions. The strategies in this book will make sense for the purpose of general reading. The advice and guidelines herein can provide many insights for the Reader ready to learn them.

However, there is no substitute for "seat in the chair" SELF-Parenting experience. There is no "fast track" that reading advanced material like this will speed your progress in any way if you are not practicing daily SELF-Parenting sessions. Your personal practice engaging as an Inner Parent with your Inner Child is the fundamental tools needed for you to access the deeper levels of this advisory material.

John K. Pollard, III
2020

TABLE OF CONTENTS

DEDICATION III

ACKNOWLEDGMENTS III

FOREWORD V

THE PURPOSE FOR THIS BOOK: 1

A BRIEF REVIEW OF THE SELF-PARENTING PARADIGM 7

THE "PROBLEM" WITH SELF-PARENTING 13

YOU ARE ALWAYS SELF-PARENTING 21

SELF-PARENTING: THE ORIGIN STORY 29

SELF-PARENTING: WHERE DID IT COME FROM? 39

SELF-PARENTING: MEET GENERIC HUMAN STUDIES 47

INTRODUCING YOUR PERSONAL WORLD 57

LET'S TALK ABOUT EMOTIONAL 71

LET'S TALK ABOUT MENTAL 83

YOUR "RELATIONAL WORLD" INTERACTING WITH OUTER PEOPLE 95

A BRIEF OUTLINE OF HOW RELATIONSHIPS WORK 103

HOW SELF-PARENTING BENEFITS YOUR "OUTER" RELATIONSHIPS 127

SELF-PARENTING IN YOUR "FINANCIAL WORLD" 139

MANAGING MONEY IN YOUR FINANCIAL WORLD 149

WHAT IF MONEY WAS A BOARD GAME? 161

THE SINKS: MONEY ACTION ACCOUNTS 173

THE SECOND-BEST SELF-PARENTING MONEY TIP OF ALL TIME 187

YOU HAVE YOUR MONEY MAGNET, NOW WHAT? 199

THE EARNING SINK: 209

MONEY COMING IN 209

A BRIEF INTRODUCTION TO GENERIC HUMAN STUDIES (GHS) 221

THE NINE WORDS OF GENERIC HUMAN STUDIES 229

ABOUT THE AUTHOR 237

Introduction:
The Purpose for This Book:

Introduction: The Purpose for This Book

For those of you on this journey, you need to know something. SELF-Parenting represents the exact center of your existence. It defines the very core of your being and represents the origin of your human self-awareness. There is nothing you do, feel, or believe that is not driven by your internal thinking based on your SELF-Parenting Style. When you cognize that SELF-Parenting is the core operating system of your human bio computer, then you will be able to work with SELF-Parenting at the depth this book describes.

This book provides a concise, yet comprehensive roadmap to the basic elements of being human. It acts as an owners' manual to outline three core aspects of your life with a completely original understanding of what it means to be human. This is not just about your day-to-day SELF-Parenting; it's about the totality of your life and the purpose you chose to be born on this planet, to your parents, in your culture.

The journey you are on does not end anytime soon. There is no point during your lifetime when you are going to stop SELF-Parenting. Even if you chose to end the daily practice as described in the earlier works, you will remain a SELF-Parenting person only with less conscious awareness. I wish you the best of success understanding both "the big picture" within this book as well as the many nitty gritty specifics that are included along the way.

As mentioned in the foreword, if this book coincidently happens to be your first introduction to the concept of SELF-Parenting, you need to know this is an advanced text. It's being provided for those who have already been practicing daily sessions for at least a five-year period or more.

SELF-Parenting For LIFE:

Your best introduction to SELF-Parenting are the books mentioned in the foreword. They contain the "how to" specifics of this method that you need to get started. Even reading the "blue book" before reading the "yellow book" has created confusion for readers. It would be like reading about calculus before learning algebra.

Personally, I have been consciously SELF-Parenting every day since February of 1986. This means with pen on paper, seat in the chair, following the exact protocols as presented in *SELF-Parenting: The Complete Guide to Your Inner Conversations*.

Originally SELF-Parenting was not meant to be a psychological text, but rather a philosophical concept. As a direct result of the distinguished psychologists who "borrowed these ideas," the premise of SELF-Parenting became modified and eventually adapted into what became "inner child work." Because of the "yellow book," inner child work became a fundamental tool of psychology. But SELF-Parenting is not "inner child work!" It goes way beyond this lessor understanding.

The original ideas that became the basis of SELF-Parenting came to me in 1970. In part, this book will tell this tale for the historical record. However, that was long ago, and this is now. Today's purpose is to place the concept of SELF-Parenting within the context of the next 30 years of your daily life. Its purpose is to leave clues for future generations on how valuable this knowledge is.

Before I pass, I wanted to share my deepest understandings of SELF-Parenting in the hopes that individuals reading this book forever into the future will understand it's value and importance. Use it to guide your personal growth, within this big

Introduction: The Purpose for This Book

crowded planet of competing people, places, and ideas where ideally, we all coexist with our fellow humans.

Simply understand that for human beings, SELF-Parenting is the key process by which our brain works, and by extrapolation our "mind." The thoughts and feelings created inside our brain/mind simply reflect the dynamics of our Inner Parent who is parenting our Inner Child.

Our "Inner Parent" comes from the way we were parented by our outer parents. Our "Inner Child" is the same child we were as a kid, even if we are now a 50-year-old adult. These dynamics were internalized long before we became consciously aware of this process. This simply models the natural aspect of living life universal to all human cultures. Right or wrong we absorb what our parents teach us. These teachings go deeply into our internal programming. When we need to uncover and unlearn some of the negative patterns, it can be quite challenging.

The ideal path for reading this book would be start with **SELF-Parenting: The Complete Guide to Your Inner Conversations**, as the first book to read on this topic. Part I gives a very clear description of the Inner Parent and Inner Child personalities and how they interact. Part II discusses the dynamics of Inner Conflicts and the 8 Steps for resolving them in a win/win manner.

Part III guides you through your first 3-6 months of SELF-Parenting. Over a period of six months to two years you would read and study the "blue book" and practice these understandings as you engage consciously in daily life experiences with your Inner Child.

If this book is by chance your first introduction to the topic, you are certainly welcome to read it. But key experiences within you will simply be missing that are necessary to understand what's being said. As alluded to earlier, it would be like reading an advanced book about math before ever learning the times tables.

You'll never stop SELF-Parenting. You can't stop SELF-Parenting. Every human being is already SELF-Parenting. I am not suggesting people are doing this consciously, the way practitioners do with our half-hour session. The "Inner Conversations" of SELF-Parenting typically take place just beneath your conscious awareness.

SELF-Parenting is simply how the human brain/mind works; it's not a choice. This is true for every culture, language, and collection of living human beings. All the people living on this earth in their own countries, cultures, and environments are SELF-Parenting based on the way they were brought up within their individual circumstances.

The SELF-Parenting process was installed in your brain before you were aware of it growing up. It's been that way since mankind began. All animals are taught how to think, feel, and act by the parenting they receive from their outer parents. Basically, this book is presented as a guide to help you understand all the ways it permeates and influences your daily existence.

Your goal as a student of life, is to become as consciously aware of your SELF-Parenting style as possible, so that you can live the most fully consciously ideal life possible for your remaining years as a SELF-Parenting Practitioner.

One of the key points made within these pages is that having a conscious and aware SELF-Parenting style is not the only thing you need to strive for in this world. You also need to know how relationships work. Before most people become conscious of

Introduction: The Purpose for This Book

their SELF-Parenting style it turns out they are floating through life in a sea of relationships. Until they learn how relationships work, they live at the effect of the way others treat them.

As you mature and gain enough conscious awareness to make your own decisions in life, then your happiness can be somewhat under your control. As you enter young adulthood you begin to truly decide your own path in life.

Please consider these words carefully.

As I will explain throughout this book, SELF-Parenting is the one thing you are doing 100% of the time. You, the Inner Parent, can "control and use it" regardless of your outer circumstances, by cooperating with your Inner Child.

It is the core motivator for who you are, and there is no deeper core process that will be discovered one day that will replace this understanding. This has always been true, is true now, and will be true forever in humanity's future.

Chapter 1:

A Brief Review of the SELF-Parenting Paradigm

Chapter 1: A Brief Review of the SELF-Parenting Paradigm

Your default style of (raw) SELF-Parenting comes from your parents or early caretakers. Whoever they were, whatever your specific or unique circumstances, the conversation that occurs second-by-second within your mind was established by the way these outer parents/caretakers took care of you as an infant. Combine your early childhood upbringing along with the unique social circumstances in which you were born, and you have the personal style of SELF-Parenting you experience today.

If you were brought up in a happy, loving family, you have an excellent chance of enjoying a happy loving SELF-Parenting experience. This typically means you are so content with life that you seldom look for self-help ideas because you don't have the need.

If you were brought up by negative outer parents, or in difficult environmental situations such as extreme poverty or being orphaned at an early age, the chances of your having a positive SELF-Parenting style are much less likely. If this is your situation then you are a person who has tried so many self-help methods to solve your various problems that you could write your own book.

Upbringing and outer circumstances however are not the final determinate of your SELF-Parenting style. You do not have to remain stuck in whatever programming life gave you growing up. Once you become a conscious adult, let's say from the age of 18 onward, you have the ability to become a positive Inner Parent no matter how negative your upbringing or rough and tumble your childhood may have been.

If you choose to and are willing to apply even a small consistent daily effort (30 mins), you can create a positive working relationship with your Inner Child. Even a person with the worst-case scenario can create the beginnings of a turnaround within 3 months of properly conducted SELF-Parenting.

Here is something you might not have realized. Your internal SELF-Parenting is actually a relationship. It is a relationship between two selves. One "self" is your Inner Parent typically referred to as the ego. The other "self" is your Inner Child, classically identified as your feelings/emotions.

After all, you hear two voices in your head, so one voice is talking to the other, and the other voice is listening and responding back. These two internal personalities are interacting with each other all day long. This takes place so easily and internally, that the average person rarely has awareness of this consciously. Usually it takes some trauma or deep hurt for a person to start digging more deeply into understanding how their mind operates on this level.

If you learn how to evaluate this internal relationship as if taking place on a seesaw, you will understand this interaction on a very useful level. Allow me to share a helpful analogy from the book, **How Relationships Work** to illustrate this point.

All relationships (even your Inner Parent/Inner Child relationship) take place: in an Environment, on a Seesaw structure, between Two Copartners. In this case the environment is inside your head, the seesaw structure is your left brain/right brain and your two copartners are the internal conscious personalities of your Inner Parent and Inner Child.

Chapter 1: A Brief Review of the SELF-Parenting Paradigm

One important thing to note about relationships. They have four possible outcomes. To briefly summarize, they are:

- Lose/Lose
- Win/Lose
- Lose/Win
- Win/Win

This means that any two-people interacting in any outer relationship can have one of these four options of winning or losing depending on how their relationship communication plays out. This also works the same way with your internal SELF-Parenting relationship.

More detail is coming later, but the point here is that within your consciousness as a SELF-Parenting practitioner, your mind can move through any of these 4 states within seconds.

As you begin to consciously self-parent, you will start getting glimpses of how each of these various relationship outcomes make you feel inside. Eventually, as you gain experience practicing the half-hour sessions, you will learn to strive for a Win/Win relationship with your Inner Child as much of the time as possible.

It's possible to have a 100% Win/Win relationship with your Inner Child. It's also not easy depending where you started, but daily gains with big leaps in awareness are built into the system.

Chapter 2:
The "Problem" with SELF-Parenting

Chapter 2: The "Problem" with SELF-Parenting

SELF-Parenting is great, it is amazing, it's the key to your inner happiness. Unfortunately, it is not the end all and be all of human life. This is important to understand because it could be construed that if your SELF-Parenting was 100% positive then everything in your life would be perfect. This is the mistake many positive mental attitude (PMA) people make and I would like to clarify this point right from the beginning.

Yes, you can be 100% happy while everyone around you is miserable. However the totality of life experience needs more than this for your overall life to be enjoyable. A successful human life means that you will participate in many successful (win/win) outer relationships.

Let's assume your SELF-Parenting is really good, and within your own self you are completely happy most of the time. That's great and only possible because you have jurisdiction over both sides of your seesaw. If either your Inner Parent or Inner Child are unhappy, you can use win/win problem solving to clear it up.

Here is the problem. Much of your "outer happiness" revolves around your relationships with others. As it turns out, according to the GHS Seesaw Theory of Relationships, you are only one half of an outer relationship. This is a very important point to understand.

Let's take a Friend/Friend relationship. You and your friend like to do things together. What happens if your friend wants to go to a movie and you want to go for a hike? These are incompatible activities if you only have a certain amount of time to be together. You can't do both at the same time.

In your outer relationship, you have to resolve this "conflict" with your outer friend. How you resolve this outer conflict with your friend determines your relationship satisfaction based on the four outcomes of success as previously mentioned. Here they are again:

- Lose/Lose
- Win/Lose
- Lose/Win
- Win/Win

You may still want to go for a hike but spending time with your friend may be even more important to you, so watching a movie is your most acceptable option at the moment. In this case, it is a "lose" for you since watching a movie isn't really interacting time with your friend.

Let's say your friend is willing to go for a hike with you, even though he/she really wants to see this movie. This could be interpreted as a "win" for you and a "lose" for him/her.

This is a simple example, and you will encounter many more complex illustrations of exactly this kind of conflict in your outer relationships. Maybe you and your friend will get into an argument about it all and create a "lose/lose" result where you don't do either.

One way to resolve this is after discussing the situation and both clarifying your needs, you mutually decide to do one activity now, and the other the next time. This would be the "win/win" option. And certainly, resolving any outer conflicts with good friends is much easier than with the other 11 categories of relationships

Here's the problem with outer relationships. Not only are you only one-half of the seesaw, you have no control over the other half. In reality, this means you are completely reliant on the

Chapter 2: The "Problem" with SELF-Parenting

other half of your relationship seesaw for the success of the relationship. If your friend decides to not do anything at all, there's nothing you can do about it; and vice versa. The only consolation you might have is that your copartner is also 100% reliant on you in your relationship. If you mess up the relationship, there's nothing the other person can do.

Outer relationships are tricky as a topic all to themselves and there are many more details in *How Relationships Work*. A second book of deeper understandings is now available called, *How Communication Works*. This addresses the Sender/Receiver flows of relationships. We know a lot about relationships, but it still has to be applied.

As far as outer relationships go, with this book, you are here to extrapolate the success of your personal SELF-Parenting relationship. Basically, your job as the Inner Parent is to strive for Win/Win relationship outcomes with your Inner Child. These experiences and achievements can then be applied to your half of your outer relationship seesaws. It's the same process, but when you achieve it with your inner selves you are on a deeper depth of energy. You can be happy within yourself even with failed relationships, but it's lonely.

You could have the exact scenario above except taking place within your own internal conversations. Your Inner might want to go for a hike. Your Inner Parent might want to see a movie (or vice versa). If you don't resolve this SELF-Parenting interaction in a win/win way, it's very possible you will become so upset and conflicted internally that you won't do either.

In other words, if your Inner Parent is unhappy OR your Inner Child is unhappy, you are not going to be completely happy. Both selves must be happy for you to achieve a successful Win/Win relationship. Thankfully, you are 100% in charge of your SELF-Parenting Style, and you can always have a win/win relationship once you study and apply the 8 Steps of Inner Conflict Resolution.

What we find happening for the Intermediate to Advance Practitioners is that their "inner happiness" starts to conflict with their "outer happiness" i.e. relationships in a way that can no longer be ignored or avoided. After about 2-5 years of quality SELF-Parenting, your typical inner conflicts become a thing of the past. From thereon it's basically about outer relationships and money, as you'll see further along in the book.

In the big scheme of things, depending on your personal circumstances, you will need to work out for yourself just how important your own personal needs rank as opposed to the greater needs of your family, community and culture.

This type of understanding begins to become more important after you've practiced about 2-5 years of conscious SELF-Parenting following all the protocols. From this time forward, you will typically have a very solid understanding of your personal needs as experienced between your Inner Parent and Inner Child.

You will have spent much time resolving inner conflicts over situations and problems that were within your control. In other words, you will come to know your inner selves quite well. You will know what you like and don't like, and you will become less willing to compromise in non-essential areas just for the sake of compromise. You will certainly become motivated to define and defend your most important inner needs and values when challenged by outer circumstances.

We live in the "outer world." For example, most of us need to work. Where you work, who you work for, and what you do all

Chapter 2: The "Problem" with SELF-Parenting

day can require a lot of compromise from what might be your own inner desires.

You may have to deal with a boss, coworkers, or employees that you don't necessarily like. You might have to live in a place that is not your ideal situation. You might have to endure outer hardships and sacrifice under difficult situations to achieve a greater goal. Many people simply call this "life." But you are becoming more conscious now and constantly reassessing your priorities.

Basically, life is the ultimate teacher. No matter how protected or coddled a life you might attempt to create for yourself, life has a way of putting you in challenging circumstances that force you to use your SELF-Parenting skills to extricate and manage your way.

The people you choose to live with, hang out with, work with, along with your neighborhood are all choices within your SELF-Parenting decision-making abilities. As you strive to build a life based on your personal needs, it sometimes seems that everyone and everything conspires to get in your way, even when there's no reason!

Even if you are 100% happy within your own half of your various outer seesaws of life, you will encounter many trials and tribulations based on the fact that other people are either not consciously SELF-Parenting Or, they may be actively trying to manipulate you, rip you off, or somehow make trouble in some way just because that's how they operate their lives.

Even if you keep your wits and morals about you and consciously SELF-Parent to a very high degree, your outer life can present situations that are out of your control with which you have to deal as best possible. I know this for fact because I've had some of the craziest circumstances happen to me that could ever be imagined, most of it impossible, yet I still had to deal with it whether I liked it or not. The good news is that these kinds of experiences often bring about the most rapid personal growth if handled correctly.

One example of this could be a natural disaster. My house burnt down in a Malibu fire. Some arsonist lit a fire 40 miles away which the Santa Ana winds blew right into my perfect beachside home. Lucky me, through the process of conscious SELF-Parenting, I was able to rebuild and make it even more perfect. And yet not 15 years later I lost it again right under my nose based on an outer relationship, without me knowing somehow.

So, beware, there are no guarantees in life. Decisions you make consciously from one side of an outer seesaw can be totally upset and turned around by your copartners on the other side of your various seesaws.

Through the practice of conscious SELF-Parenting you can manage to achieve win/win solutions on the inside between both inner selves. But in the outer world, there are too many variables that are simply out of your control.

Chapter 3:
You Are Always Self-Parenting

Chapter 3: You Are Always SELF-Parenting

The most important detail which most people miss still to this day, is that everyone is SELF-Parenting. Not consciously of course, most people have little awareness of the quantity or quality of their inner conversations. They certainly do not realize how their internal inner conversations are identical to the way they were parented by their parents.

Even if you decide SELF-Parenting is a bunch of hogwash and has no bearing on you or your life in any way, you are still using the described process of SELF-Parenting to make this assessment. Hopefully this logic is easy to understand because if so, you will be able to:

1) Do something about it
2) Realize it's in your best interest to be as conscious as possible about how your mind works
3) Begin to understand how and why other people make the decisions they do

You can't really do anything about other people's SELF-Parenting style. You can recognize it. You can make suggestions. You can work around it. You can compensate for it in a number of various ways. But the reality is that each person is solely and completely responsible for his/her own SELF-Parenting style (after the age of 18).

What this means for you is that you are fully capable of creating your own happiness. What it could mean for others is if this person is someone who respects your opinion, maybe he/she will consider beginning the practice of daily conscious SELF-Parenting. But even this is not something you can depend on.

If you are an outer parent you are certainly contributing at least one-half to your outer child's inner SELF-Parenting, especially when they are younger. But eventually your child grows up, becomes socialized within his/her culture, and begins interacting with peers at school, watching television, listening to music, advertising, and creating their own life.

Eventually each child adopts and settles into their unique, yet also their "default," SELF-Parenting style. Let's say that turning the age of 18 signifies a transition from child to adult in his/her life. Each person from this time forward can be assigned ownership to his/her own ongoing internal SELF-Parenting results based on the 4 options mentioned earlier.

We live in an increasingly complicated world where communication and programming bombards us from all sides. Depending on the internal tendencies of each individual, they may read or hear one sentence from somewhere that changes their life forever. Whereas a sibling sitting right next to them never saw or heard this sentence in the first place. Each of us is a unique individual and we each bring our own specific predispositions and nuances to our current upbringing.

You certainly know families where all the siblings are similar and other families where every child is completely different. As humans, we live in a big blender of DNA and past experiences. Even if you are brought up by the same parents, if you were born in a different decade than your siblings, your outer parenting experience will be completely different thus contributing to your personal SELF-Parenting point of view.

Regardless of any of this, YOU, the person reading this book, are SELF-Parenting right now; night and day, 168 hours a week, 24-7, year in and year out, from your first dawning of awareness until your last dying breath. What you do with this information and how you proceed from this moment forward is up to you and you alone.

Chapter 3: You Are Always SELF-Parenting

My recommendation is to become as consciously aware of this process as possible. I've been doing it daily for 30 plus years, and my SELF-Parenting is still as fresh a process for me now as the day I started. I still have "issues." They are very likely different from yours if you're just starting out. I am reminded of the well-known Einstein quote, "Do not worry about your difficulties in mathematics. I can assure you mine are still greater."

Which is not to say that my S/P problems are greater, they are simply more nuanced. I still remain vigilant as the Inner Parent and pay close and constant attention to my Inner Child. I must be ever watchful not to roadblock my Inner Child or take over daily decision-making and life choices that would be better served by win-win cooperation between my two inner selves.

There may be a point in time where "enlightenment" takes the place of conscious SELF-Parenting. Lord knows I've been working to make this transition. Since the age of 18 I began high-quality meditation methods with renown and respected teachers. Throughout all my efforts, it still remains that conscious SELF-Parenting has been the best approach for me to process all my efforts to gain higher consciousness.

It's part of the motivation for writing this book, to let you know that SELF-Parenting is a fundamental key to living life as a human. I have been consistently and always SELF-Parenting, whether I liked it or not, and I've given 100% of my best efforts to be consistent with daily half hour sessions regardless of whatever else was occurring in my life. This is the same recommendation I'm advising for you, on your behalf, for your best possible outcomes with this practice.

What you do is up to you; how you live your life, what your goals and needs are, what it takes to make you happy. You sit in the driver seat. As the Inner Parent, assuming you live in a free society, you have multiple choices. All I can tell you is, based on my experience with a multitude of consciousness growth techniques, SELF-Parenting remains a central understanding of the mind which you can rely on with confidence.

Throughout this book I share many of these best practice techniques and explain how they contributed to my positive SELF-Parenting style. SELF-Parenting is certainly not the only game in town. There exists a plethora of psychological systems that claim to be the answer to all problems. And many of them, if practiced diligently, could very much be the answer to your current situation.

Speaking for the whole of humanity and including all the potential mental problems that could exist, SELF-Parenting is a core understanding that will serve you well for the entirety of your life. Perhaps you successfully practice or follow another method or mental understanding that makes you completely happy. If you shared it with me, I could ultimately show you how using the system you follow enables you to be a positive Inner Parent to your Inner Child, simply using different methods and terminology.

Whatever makes you happy in life will ultimately have to balance your ego aspirations and your emotional needs. Mankind has evolved a surplus of methods, philosophies, and religions to satisfy the numerous varieties of human experience and existence. SELF-Parenting just represents one very concise model, using simple language based on universal human dynamics, that explains the basic issues of mind as applies to humans of all cultures and races.

You may be 100% completely happy with your life. You may never have heard of or encountered the concept of SELF-

Chapter 3: You Are Always SELF-Parenting

Parenting. Your philosophy, religion, and who you are may just naturally be all you need to be the happiest person on earth.

But one day, if something rocks your world, and all of a sudden you are facing the doubts, trials, and tribulations so many of us experience as humans, conscious SELF-Parenting provides a firm foundation to begin your quest back to your happy state.

Chapter 4:

Self-Parenting: The Origin Story

Chapter 4: SELF-Parenting: The Origin Story

Next, I'm presenting the SELF-Parenting Origin Story, for your understanding and review. I have never told the story to this level of detail before. After 50 years I'd like it to be known and have it on record for future generations.

I use one basic method to evaluate when someone says they invented something, came up with an idea, or achieved a certain state or discovery. Let's call this their "Origin Story."

An excellent example of this comes from the movie *Working Girl*. It recounts the adventures of an aspiring office pool secretary who wants to join the executive ranks. As the new secretary, she tells her female boss about a great idea she came up with for one of her clients, a business mogul.

She tells her boss the idea, which is for a specific client to take an ownership position in radio not TV, as an example of how enthused she is to become an executive. However, her self-centered boss plans to steal the idea and is clearly going to present it to the business mogul as "her idea," so she can get the credit.

Spoiler Alert: The secretary finds out about the plans of her boss. And she is able to tell the business mogul that it was her idea, not her bosses.

The climax of the movie comes when the business owner, after being pitched this great idea by the big boss, decides to ask her, "How did you come up with this idea to purchase radio stations? It wasn't exactly an idea floating around that anyone else ever suggested."

At which point the boss character stumbles through a story that does not make any sense and was clearly made up. It was sort of a "I'll get back to you on that one" answer.

When the business owner asked the young staffer how she came up with the idea, it was a totally different explanation. She outlined how she had "read an article in the paper and realized his company could meet their needs better through purchasing radio than TV." She presented a very logical scenario that described how her insightful cognition led to this great idea. After this it was very clear whose original idea it was.

Basically, it's up to the listener to decide how an origin story meets his/her need to validate what the teller is saying and if it makes sense to them. This is my "origin story" of how SELF-Parenting came into being.

During the summer of 1970 I was studying with Maharishi Mahesh Yogi to become one of his TM initiators. This was the east coast training in Poland Springs. I had a roommate named Wally and we got to know each other over the month. I would say something casual about wanting to do something and he would make the statement, "Let George do it." This was so strange to me that after he said it several times I inquired as to his meaning. He explained that he had read a book about the Huna Religion, called *The Secret Science at Work*, by Max Freedom Long.

He detailed how Max had heard tales of the amazing exploits of the Kahunas, who were the medicine men of the Hawaiian culture. They could do things like walk on fire, throw sticks that would be charged with energy to knock out their enemies, and perform healings and "miracles" that were not scientifically explainable.

Max made it his life purpose to discover how the Kahuna priests achieved these secret techniques which were never revealed even with other members of the tribe, much less the white people who had recently invaded the Hawaiian Islands.

Chapter 4: SELF-Parenting: The Origin Story

Through a colleague of his at a Hawaiian museum, he learned some early hints, and then through hard work and studying the Hawaiian language for more clues, he pieced together his theory of the core principles that enabled the Kahunas to perform these feats. It basically goes as follows.

The aboriginal religion of the ancient Hawaiians divided a person into three selves, which Max called the Middle Self, the Low Self, and the High Self. There were names given in Hawaiian, but he translated these to English terms to make it simple.

The Middle Self was the conscious self, the ego, what most people would consider the personality of a person. This is the self who makes decisions, does whatever the person decides, and lives a normal life. This self would be very typical and recognized by every culture. Some call it the conscious mind. Western psychology calls it the ego. But it was the addition of the two other selves that provided the key to the dynamics of the Kahuna's abilities.

Max described a second personality applied by the Kahunas he called the "Low Self." This self was more animalistic, more emotional. There was an element of inability to control this self. It had its own personality and will. It was not under the control of the Middle Self unless measures were taken. But there was much more to understand about this "lower self."

This self was described as controlling the core bodily energies of the person, their deep emotional desires as well as memory. This was not a logical self but a willful energetic self that needed to be dealt with and controlled or else it could get out of hand.

If this self somehow got the wrong idea, it could lead the person down the path to getting sick, or acting out in anger, etc. It could be vengeful and act independently and completely at odds with the person's own conscious self as the ego, or even act against other members of society in which it was living. There was also a third self.

This third self, called the High Self, was said to be a spiritual self, known as the Utter Trustworthy Parents, as it was a combination of both male and female spiritual qualities. This self was not God, per se, but acted as each person's personal representative to its higher spiritual realms.

The Higher Self was linked by a cord, called the Aka Cord to the Low Self which was essentially connected just like an umbilical cord. The Middle Self was connected to the Low Self by virtue of sharing and living together in the same body.

The key to the Huna system, as discovered and defined by Max Freedom Long, was the way in which the three selves would combine and interact to construct a prayer by which to accomplish the goals that the individual human being wanted.

In very simple terms, the lower two selves, the Middle and the Low Self were responsible to live in the body, and to interact and manage their ongoing day-to-day concerns of being human. It was the job/mission of the lower two selves to get along with each other and to work out their basic differences during their various life activities.

The High Self is there to guide the overall long-term direction of the human being for the purpose of directing and fulfilling the life purpose for which they were born. However, the Higher Selves do not bother much about the day-to-day activities of the lower two selves, unless there is a major problem.

The "ideal life" for the three selves was the successful combination of their different roles and personalities. The role of the

Chapter 4: SELF-Parenting: The Origin Story

Middle Self is to guide and protect the Low Self. The role of the Low Self is to provide the energy and enthusiasm for living. The High Self provides long term guidance to fulfil each person's life purpose.

Essentially the High Self would stay out of the day-to-day lives of the 2-lower selves, letting them do their thing. The lower two selves were tasked with the responsibility to create and work out their basic human activities without interference. Human's on this earth enjoy free will to do whatever they like basically.

However, the High Self can be contacted and asked for special favors or guidance if requested correctly. The key to the success of the Kahuna priests as discovered by Max was, they had evolved a form of prayer by which they could successfully and powerfully make this contact. Max figured out how the Kahunas made their prayers and thus gained access to their "secret powers."

Basically, the Higher Self could grant the lower two selves anything they asked for, as long as it was for their highest good. But a certain formula is required to evoke the prayer. The two lower selves must cooperatively combine their strengths for the prayer to work.

The Middle Self is tasked with forming a very clear mental picture of what is being requested. The Low Self's contribution is to provide the energy to serve as the fuel for the successful fulfillment of the request. The High Self provides the request, as long as there was enough energy sent along with a clear image/idea of what was desired.

When the Middle Self and Low Self pool their two distinct energies correctly, they send their pictured prayer request (along with the required energy) up through the Aka Cord connecting them to the Higher Selves. Once the Higher Selves receive this clear picture of what is requested along with the required energy, and assuming it's compatible with the highest good, it delivers the prayer result directly to the lower Two Selves.

Thus, when a Kahuna wanted to heal someone, he would create a clear picture of the healed state, generate energy provided by the Low Self, and send this to the High Self along the Aka Cord, and it would be delivered.

Because this prayer method required clear communication between the lower 2 Selves for creating their prayer together, Max also developed the use of a pendulum to communicate with "George" which was his pet name for the Low Self.

It was pretty clear that much of the time the Middle Self didn't know or wasn't clear about what was going on from the Lower Self's side of the seesaw. Using a pendulum, Max worked out a way his Middle Self could ask "George" his Lower Self, his opinion about various topics under consideration.

If the pendulum went one direction, it was a "yes" answer. If it went the other way, it was a "no." Now the Middle Self had a way to communicate with the Low Self to make sure they were both in agreement as to what was being requested. If the Middle Self wanted one thing and the Low Self wanted something else, then the prayer could not be delivered correctly due to the conflict. And thus, the prayer would not be answered.

When the Middle Self was unsure of the low self's opinion, it could ask questions and clarify where George stood on any particular issue. Once the agreement on what to ask for in cooperation between the two lower selves was established, it was then possible to send the prayer requests up to the High Self for fulfillment.

Chapter 4: SELF-Parenting: The Origin Story

When Max Freedom Long began to teach this prayer method to others, the term "let George do it" became the shorthand way for Max to describe how easy the technique was, once you were in touch with the true needs and desires of your Low Self. The premise being that the Middle Self did not need to "will" or "concentrate" or use any effort at all to get whatever it wanted. It only needed to form a clear picture of what was desired in his/her mind.

The actual energy for accomplishing the goal was supplied by the Low Self. The phrase "let George do it" meant the Low Self was responsible for the heavy lifting of providing the emotional energy which was its ability. There was no need for the Middle Self (ego) to struggle or stress about it. Once the prayer was sent to the Higher Selves for fulfillment, everything would happen in an effortless positive manner, assuming it was for the Highest Good.

Once Max worked out these fundamentals, he began teaching this prayer method to others. He formed groups, wrote books and was very successful at the time. Many people using these methods became very effective at achieving whatever it was they wanted.

My roommate Wally was a great example. He was amazingly able to do all kinds of things by "letting George do it." I on the other hand was having a dreadful time trying to get my "George" to do anything, which I can tell you was very frustrating.

Long story short when I returned to Los Angeles, I went to the Bodhi tree bookstore and bought my own copy of *The Secret Science at Work* (one of Max's early books on this topic) which I studied profusely. I learned the pendulum technique and I did my best to follow all the procedures. But still I was feeling very frustrated that I could not manifest the kinds of desires and needs that my friend Wally could do so effortlessly.

After completing my training with Maharishi in the fall of 70, I even went to Hawaii (taking my copy of the Huna book) to the island of Kauai. I was following some sense of destiny that I could learn more about the Huna system there. I can tell you that I was still not very successful even though I enjoyed Hawaii.

I do have one story of a successful prayer result that relates to this time. In Hawaii, I knew who I wanted to stay with, but I did not have his address. I knew he lived in Kauai, but that was basically it. I just hopped on the plane.

On the flight over there I realized I better do something a bit more concrete to find my friend, so I made a prayer request sitting on the plane. I offered a lot of energy from my Low Self while at the same time I sent a strong request to find my friend along the Aka Cord to my Higher Self. It was a very distinct and powerful prayer as it turned out.

Being rather penniless at the time I was walking out of the Lihue Airport and found myself on a desolate road surrounded by what appeared to be sugarcane. Remember this was the summer of 1971 by now.

I stuck out my thumb to hitchhike into town and the first car that stopped to pick me up had my friend sitting in the front seat. As his friend was driving, he didn't even know it was me until I got in. So, I considered this a successful prayer result, maybe my best ever.

Chapter 5:

Self-Parenting: Where Did It Come From?

Chapter 5: SELF-Parenting: Where Did It Come From?

For a time, I concentrated very heavily on practicing the Huna Prayer Method as it came to be called. And just a side note, the term Huna was Max Freedom Long's original word. No Hawaiians used this term, certainly not the remaining few "true Kahunas" of which there may have been only one or two legitimate ones remaining. They did not make themselves known at all to the public at large. Their religion was a collection of secret methods, even from their own tribal members.

Max had long moved away from Hawaii and was living in Southern California. Many years later some Hawaiians started using the term Huna like they made it up when they simply stole Max's name and ideas. The funny part was, they made a pitiful attempt to pretend that they were the legitimate "Huna" people from the islands, which of course they were not. Remember the Origin Story idea.

From Hawaii, I moved to Kansas City in the fall of 1971 (to begin Chiropractic school) at which time I contacted Max and began to receive his Huna newsletters which were clearly a labor of love, mimeographed typed pages stapled together. But truly, I was still having a heck of a time trying to get the Huna prayer method to work to my satisfaction. It was this building frustration that finally provided the key to the "discovery" of SELF-Parenting.

One day I was reviewing all the characteristics of the Middle and Lower Selves, yet again trying to figure out what I was doing wrong. The spark of insight came when I noticed that the Middle Self traits sounded strangely similar to those of a parent. Max had listed about 10 traits of the Middle Self and they all looked and sounded as to how a parent should be.

Then, with a sense of growing excitement, when I looked at the Low Self traits, they indeed resembled exactly a description of how a "natural child" would act. So, I thought to myself, "I'm going to study outer parenting methods" with the idea that there must be some established principles of outer parenting that somebody had already figured out. There must be some information as to how a positive outer parent could create a good relationship with his/her outer child.

Maybe it was luck but the very first book I studied for outer parenting was ***P.E.T: Parent Effectiveness Training*** by Thomas Gordon. Low and behold everything he said fit exactly into the Middle Self and Low Self paradigm as described by Max. It was now very obvious that the Middle Self was a Parent and the Low Self was a Child. What else could I call them but Inner Parent and Inner Child?

So, my goal then became to train my Inner Parent to become skillful at using the P.E.T methods of outer parenting in what I was still calling my "inner conversations." It wasn't easy to change my Inner Parent in the beginning, but it sure did start working well. My Inner Parent was very good at road-blocking my Inner Child.

Basically, SELF-Parenting was birthed thru the combination of Max Freedom Long's Huna studies and P.E.T. outer parenting methods. Let's say the two got married and had the SELF-Parenting baby. Finally, I was able to get a handle on all the stupid and ineffective ways I was trying to get my Inner Child to do what I wanted.

When you read the 12 roadblocks from P.E.T. (actually there are 36 roadblocks) you will learn all the bad ways you can act as an Inner Parent. You will also learn all the many ways my Inner Child was resisting the ineffective parenting skills of my Inner Parent. Over time I read P.E.T. over and over and gradually changed my Inner Parent's methods from negative to positive.

Chapter 5: SELF-Parenting: Where Did It Come From?

As part of the excitement of this discovery, I started typing everything down into actual pages on something called a typewriter. By the end I had a 40-50-page manuscript that described the whole system as it was.

Eventually it was 1975 and I was living in Pasadena, Ca. Know that the S/P ideas were like a meditation idea for me. I was studying in chiropractic school which took up most of my time. Yet from the fall of 1970 to the year in 1975, I had begun using the basic dynamics of SELF-Parenting to think, plan, and achieve many of the goals I was after.

At this time it was not a discipline that I practiced daily, like I do today. It was something that I was conscious of on a daily basis and I did make it a point to tell anyone who would listen that all us humans are SELF-Parenting ourselves inside our mind.

Not only did I tell everybody I knew that I thought cared about consciousness growth, but I told them multiple times. And I have to say, not one person truly understood the concept. They would listen to me politely, but they did not "get it" with the "aha moment" like I had. It wasn't for lack of trying.

Although I never gave up telling people, I did give up on the idea of the manuscript. I put it in a drawer and basically forgot about it. I kept using the principles for myself, but my life became involved with starting a Chiropractic practice and all the various struggles that go on in life. Eventually I started doing pretty well after a lot of stops and starts and I wound up with a holistic and successful Chiropractic practice in Canoga Park, California.

By now it's 1985, and I was becoming very bored of success. I was living in a beach house in Malibu, a really nice one I might add. It was my dream home that I had created a few years earlier during a seminar where we did such things in our imagination. However, Chiropractic practice was beginning to feel routine, which for me is not good.

During my time in Hawaii as an avid surfer, I had met some crazy Australians who convinced me that Australia was the promised land. So, over the Nov/Dec 1985 holiday season I planned a trip "down under" for six weeks and wound up staying six months. Here is where the story of SELF-Parenting's subsequent birth in what I like to call the "real world" continues after its 15-year gestation period.

One evening, I was completing a late-night adventure in Maisy's Café in Neutral Bay. Lucky for me, I met 2 Aussie girls, one blond, the other brunette. They were telling me how conscious they were because they had excelled at this great Aussie Consciousness Growth seminar, which sounded suspiciously like one modelled on any of the many American ones I had taken.

They had just finished telling me how they knew everything there was to know about consciousness growth. So, I popped the question, "Would you really like to know the true secret of the consciousness growth universe?" and of course they said, "Yes."

So, as I do and had done, I explained the concept of SELF-Parenting and how we are all parenting ourselves inside our mind, etcetera, et cetera. Lo and behold these girls actually understood exactly what I was saying.

Thus two Australian women were truly the first human beings on the planet to finally understand exactly what I had been saying for so long. Not only that, they were going to put on a

Chapter 5: SELF-Parenting: Where Did It Come From?

seminar to tell all their friends. It was a Tuesday night, and by Saturday they had eight people lined up at their house and I taught the very first official SELF-Parenting class in Sydney, Australia, during Feb 1986.

Based on the pent-up joy from this experience, I rented a Mac plus computer and typed out my 40-page manuscript into Word, version 1.0. Since I was teaching and finally had some real-world students, this original manual eventually became the yellow book along with the first two weeks of questions.

It was also at this time that I started my personal daily practice of half-hour sessions of SELF-Parenting. I told myself that if I was going to be teaching now, I better be practicing what I'm preaching!

To make a long story short, I taught one more class in Sydney and spent the next 4 months writing out the full system of not only SELF-Parenting, but also something called Generic Human Studies, of which SELF-Parenting is a component part. Once I got going, I could not stop.

This was also the period when I figured out the Seesaw Analogy of Relationships, (this story is in *How Relationships Work*) which unfortunately to this day I still feel no one truly understands in the same way that no one understood SELF-Parenting before 1986. As of this writing, I am still waiting on this one.

In the summer of 1986 when I returned to the US I began looking to see if there was any way to get my manuscript published. During this investigation, I was fortunate enough to discover the community that became the Publishers Marketing Association. This also provided the perfect timing for the many inspiring publishers in this group who helped guide and prepare the book into its current form.

I also learned about a self-help group called the Adult Children of Alcoholics, who were the exact people on this planet who it turns out needed the concept of SELF-Parenting more than any others. I became a "founding member" of this group myself in Westwood, CA.

By the fall of 1986 I was being distributed by the number one publisher for the ACA community, Health Communications. and within the next year every ACA and family psychologist in California was exposed to my book.

I began teaching classes in Malibu, and even had two very prominent therapists as my students. I kind of felt I was on my way and the world was to become a better place.

Chapter 6:
Self-Parenting: Meet Generic Human Studies

Chapter 6: SELF-Parenting: Meet Generic Human Studies

Next, I am going to share some important understandings that came about in conjunction with my personal SELF-Parenting. It turns out that it's also possible to combine the methods of SELF-Parenting with other genuine outer mind/body systems to achieve amazing things. I hope as a reader of this book, you will integrate many of these suggested methods, skills, and insights into your own life.

Other psychological systems can be very informative and valuable when you apply them from the internal perspective of SELF-Parenting. They most likely use different terminology and you have to read between the lines to apply them from the SELF-Parenting point-of-view. Once you know and understand the SELF-Parenting paradigm, you will see it often in other systems using different terminology.

One example of this principle is the "Inner Game" books as I like to call them, such as *Inner Skiing*, and *Inner Tennis*" by the author Timothy Gallwey. He calls the Inner Parent "Self 1", and the Inner Child "Self 2". But his techniques are masterful if you apply them correctly from the Inner Parent point of view.

Another benefit of SELF-Parenting is that you bring additional power to your efforts when you work "on the inside." Let me use an analogy to explain. Let's say you have a very positive outer relationship on the Therapist/Client seesaw. Your therapist is great, and you are a great client. It's win/win all the way.

This kind of power gained from an "outer" relationship is "molecular" in nature. Molecular energy would be like when you burned a piece of wood and you get warmth. The molecules being transformed by the burning fuel give off heat, but a lot of energy is also dispersed from the burning action itself. Even so, the many "positive insights" you learn during your therapy session can be applied to other areas of your life.

When you work internally and directly between your Inner Parent/Inner Child, you are on what I call a "nuclear" or quantum level. If you could tap the nuclear energy from the piece of wood you were burning, you release enough energy to fuel a small city. If you have a great therapist on the "molecular level" that's really good. But when you are a great therapist to your own self on the "nuclear level", as with positive SELF-Parenting, you get 100 times the energy, 100 times the value, at 100 times a cheaper price.

Working internally at the "quantum" level of your operating system is much more powerful and sustaining than attempting to collect enough outer relationships to give you the energy required to pay for the effort to maintain them. Another advantage is you can control and enhance your own participation on the internal levels, whereas outside relationships take more effort and yield less value, although they can be easier to access.

We know by now that we all are SELF-Parenting night and day, 24-7-365. Now what? You have a life. You want a happy life. How is this possible in this day and age? Pay close attention. What I'm telling you next represents 50 years of study and experience.

I'm introducing the concept known as Generic Human Studies (GHS). This is a way for you, as a SELF-Parenting student, to apply your efforts specifically at a quantum level to all the key areas of your life. Learning how to evaluate your life using GHS, will help you from this point forward.

Generic Human Studies represents the big picture of human living. It is a Theory of Everything. You use it to identify and work for positive results in each aspect of your happiness. Once you've determined a primary area of life you wish to improve,

Chapter 6: SELF-Parenting: Meet Generic Human Studies

you can "drill down" to the most nitty-gritty details of life in this area.

If you don't correctly define the generic human area from which to begin, you can't drill down. You wind up being confused or in an area of consideration that is wrong or unrelated.

To look at the totality of your whole life and try to figure out which part to isolate and where to concentrate your energy is not easy. There are so many competing systems of living and areas of concern that the untrained individual has to climb mountains to figure out even some simple things. Many of these mountains don't have anything at the top when you get there.

As a way to solve this problem, we are going to use the following words in Generic Human Studies as tools to define your reality. It's easy to do because these words are typically used all the time in a very normal manner. All you need do is look for the deeper importance of the defined terms.

Using the GHS system your Inner Parent and Inner Child begin working with a simple set of rules from the same playbook. The joy of this system is to give you a mental shorthand to encapsulate your world. If you could summarize all of humanity's endeavors in less than one hundred words, how would you do it?

It turns out you only need twelve words. These twelve words contain everything you are going to deal with as a human whether or not you know these words. It's even easier since the first three words are summary words that encapsulate the other nine. You can start with 3 words to summarize the whole of your life's activities and begin drilling down from there. We call these the Three Worlds. Choosing from one of three more main words from this first level, you can target any and all problem areas in your life. This assessment and understanding represents a huge time shortcut.

GHS defines three major categories as a person's "worlds" in human life. These worlds represent the three core areas for which you are responsible to manage your life living as a human being with others on this planet.

Here they are so you can get used to thinking about these terms in this way. In computer programming this is called a "smart system" and is used to enhance and improve your decision making. The three terms that encapsulate your life are your:

- Personal World
- Relational World
- Financial World

Each of the three "worlds" above are further defined using three words each, totaling nine altogether. The three words that summarize your Personal World are:

1. Physical World
2. Emotional World
3. Mental World

The three words that define your Relational World are:

4. Family World
5. Social World
6. Work World

The three words that define your Financial World are:

7. Buy World
8. Sell World
9. Transfer World

Chapter 6: SELF-Parenting: Meet Generic Human Studies

Your Personal World

Your Personal World covers the following three areas all under your personal jurisdiction:

1) Your Physical body and all that goes on inside your physical body
2) Your Emotional self, as defined by your Inner Child.
3) Your Mental self, as defined by your Inner Parent

That's it! There is nothing outside these three areas of who you are that reflect your "Personal World." Your Personal World represents your concerns and no one else's. Your body, your emotions, and your mind are yours alone. Your Personal World is about you as an individual; no other person is involved.

Your body, your emotions, your mind are within you and only you. These definitions become very important and are very specific so strive to follow and internalize this information in a positive way.

Your personal world could also be called your "inner life" in that it resides totally within the perimeter of your body, your heart, and between your ears. If there were no one else on earth, you would still be living in a very active Personal World.

Your Relational World

The next area of human life which concerns you begins as soon as you start interacting with other people. This is the world in which most of us are very familiar. In GHS this category is called your Relational World.

Your Relational World has three main categories:

4) Your Family Relationships
5) Your Social Relationships
6) Your Work Relationships

You know you are dealing within your Relational World when there is another person involved. Simply by interacting with any other person, you have left your Personal World and entered your Relational World. This will be discussed more fully in the chapters on relationships.

YOUR FINANCIAL WORLD

The third area of life that is ultra-important and often missing from other self-help systems, is your Financial World. Unfortunately, your Financial World cannot be ignored or avoided as it impacts your life in such a major way.

Your Financial World has three aspects:

7) Your Buying (Spending)
8) Your Selling (Earning)
9) Your Transferring (Saving/Borrowing)

Money is important because it represents the interface by which you connect with the "real world" outside your Personal and Relational lives. As the world becomes more complicated, how, when, where, and why you spend your money has life-changing consequences.

As a SELF-Parenting practitioner, how you spend, earn and manage your saving/borrowing, is very important to your overall happiness. Money is not all that matters, like many people think, but it can't be ignored. It must be given respect as a dominant world in your life.

Chapter 6: SELF-Parenting: Meet Generic Human Studies

You must consciously manage your Financial World with SELF-Parenting care and attention or you may find yourself at the wrong end of the money equation. People and in particular Places, outside your Relational World are going to deeply care about your money and you better be prepared to manage and protect yourself from their expectations and attempts to take your money.

From now, as a student of SELF-Parenting, you are assigned to manage three important areas of your life. Again, they are:

1. Your Personal World
2. Your Relational World
3. Your Financial World

Using these terms in this way will allow you to more closely parse and identify each of these important areas of daily living when the time comes and you need it most. Adopting these simple terms with a deeper understanding will clarify your life in a way you could never imagine until you begin.

Being able to define, manage, and monitor these areas with a positive SELF-Parenting Style is the foundation for all your success as a human being. Once you have a successful life, you can frame it in whatever terms you like. But from now on we are going to evaluate and/or further define your life using the Generic Human Studies framework.

Chapter 7:
Introducing Your Personal World

Chapter 7: Introducing Your Personal World

Understand this, your Personal World involves no one else but you. Maybe you think about someone or something else, but that is you, the Inner Parent thinking. Maybe you feel about someone or something else, but that's your Inner Child feeling. If you get your foot chopped off, that's your body. If someone else gets their foot chopped off, that's their body. Get it?

Your Personal World is yours to do with whatever you like, assuming you live in a free country and not within a situation where you are severely restricted physically such as prison. Even if you live in a prison cell, your Personal World is still your Personal World. This is the one domain truly under your control. You can do with it what you will. The responsibility and control of your personal life is ultimately up to you alone.

Please understand this on a very deep level and use this information in your behalf. Why? Because bottom line this is your most prized possession on the planet given to you at your birth. Your Personal World is your jurisdiction, your responsibility; in a way, no one else really cares.

Maybe you believe that you are lucky enough to know someone outside of yourself who does actually care about your world. But if it comes down to a decision between you or them, they are going to care about themselves first. If they don't, then they are violating their own Personal World. Think of these divisions from a conceptual point of view. Here are some more details to define your body, emotions, and mind.

YOUR BODY:

Your Personal World begins with your physical body. Until you are born, nothing else exists for you or follows. Your body defines your personal space and separates you from all the other bodies out there. Anything and everything from the zone of your outer skin inward involving your 12 organ systems encompasses your body.

Your body represents your hardware in a computer analogy. If your hardware is not working properly, your software has no chance to operate correctly. Without your body, you can't have emotions or a mind. Your body is the stage upon which your emotions and mind perform. Having a functional body is essential for your emotional and mental health.

In reality, all three aspects of your Personal World are interconnected. Technically, it's not really possible to separate the body from the emotions and the mind, even though we talk about them as separate. However, from the perspective of your Personal World, your body is considered to be only one part.

Something else to know about the human body is there are a variety of different models. I'm going to use a car analogy here. A car has 4 wheels, a steering wheel, motor, tires, etc. You can call this a generic car. However, there are many makes and models of cars, from the cheapest, least technology based, to the ultimate standards of materials and engineering.

If you drive a less expensive car, say some basic model, you do have a car. However, it may not be the best and strongest car on the road. If you have a late model Mercedes car, then you have a better car than another company's basic model.

However, your success with any car is ultimately determined by how well you maintain it. If you are careful and follow best practices, any modern car will last and run for a long time. If you never maintain your car and just drive it into the ground, any car, even of the topmost quality, will fail long before it's time. Now let's connect this idea to the human body.

Chapter 7: Introducing Your Personal World

A generic human body has two eyes, arms, legs, a digestive tract, etc. But some human bodies are built with stronger and more resilient materials than others. Some bodies have strong bulky muscles, others have long wiry muscles. Some bodies come with excellent eyesight, others not so much. Your personal body probably has some good aspects compared to others and maybe some lessor aspects. We can say on average that our bodies are born as equals with lots of variations.

One thing is true of all bodies. If you maintain your body carefully and completely, it will last longer and function better barring accidental injury. In my life, I believe I was given a more basic model body, but I have done my best to maintain, finetune, and upgrade my body as much as possible. Probably because my body was not the best, it's been a priority for me since an early age.

During my lifetime, I've met many people who were born gifted with genetic bodies vastly superior to mine. It was frustrating competing with them in the outside world based on the effortlessness at which they seemed to excel. Yet many of these same friends who enjoyed these bodies have had these same bodies retired to the morgue for the lack of their owner's care.

There's a built-in paradox for people born with extremely strong and healthy bodies. Because they feel so great in a natural way with so little effort, they don't focus on the maintenance aspects. They simply enjoy the life-affirming qualities of endurance, resilience, and strength until they run their bodies into the ground.

Someone with a basic type human body is going to start wondering how to fix something going wrong with their body early in life. Having early bodily symptoms can help in at least 2 ways. One, it can lead you into a long-term approach of preventative health care. Two, early symptoms (and their corrective approach) prevent you from going downhill so far that you create enough damage to pass the point of no return. Thus, having the earlier symptoms of a weaker body can mean a longer life than someone with a strong and powerful body who is able to sustain years of damage, only to develop symptoms at the last stage before breakdown.

If you are reading this with a "basic" body, then you may be thinking, "Yeah, that's me. This so explains why I care about health so much." If you have more the Mercedes type body, you may be thinking, "What a wimp. That guy should just get it together." In which case, you are probably missing my point.

Understand that your physical brain and nervous system are the hardware aspect of your emotions and mind. Physical problems with your brain or nervous system can easily impact the way you feel and think. One obvious example would be if you had a 4-inch nail pounded into your brain with a hammer. You would notice this and probably not feel that good about the experience. Another is that an infinitesimal amount of hallucinogen can create thoughts and feelings you never knew existed.

Unfortunately, common environmental factors can affect body hardware for every living human. Some examples are toxic chemicals, noise pollution, lack of sleep, missing or incomplete nutrition, "pinched nerves", and exhausted glands that create hormonal problems.

Medical literature recounts numerous examples of physical injury to a person's brain or nervous system that caused a dramatic change in the person's "emotions" or "mind." One clear example is a stroke, another is severe arthritis. Just the level of air/ground pollution in many cities impacts your physical well-being which takes its toll on your emotional and mental health.

Chapter 7: Introducing Your Personal World

Your brain and nervous system are necessary to your mind in the same way that computer hardware needs to be "healthy" for computer software to work properly.

A known aspect of your physical brain is that you actually have two separate "brains" that operate in tandem to create what most people call the brain. They are called lobes and there is a Left Lobe and a Right Lobe. Each has specific strengths and functions that act independently of each other but in the healthy person they also connect and integrate their activities.

Although separate from each other anatomically, these lobes are joined by a bridge of nerves called the corpus callosum. They are also connected by neural circuits in so many ways we don't even understand as yet, but it's interesting to note the 2-brain structure.

From the SELF-Parenting point of view, your left brain represents the ego, conscious self, the basis of your Inner Parent. It controls the right side of your body and is involved in the "logical functions" like math and science. It is the rational side and likes to follow instructions and figure things out logically step by step.

Your right brain controls the left side of your body and is associated with holistic creativity and artistic activities. It is the intuitive side and solves problems by grasping the big picture. I'm being simplistic here for the purpose of communication, but this mapping of the brain is beyond dispute. Brain neuroscience has been a growing field of knowledge for over 40 years.

Everything you learn about nutrition, diet, digestion, sleep, exercise, relaxation, and even meditation are physical methods to impact your physical body to influence and affect your emotional/mental function. In my experience as a Doctor of

Chiropractic, I have witnessed many people healed from their emotional/mental symptoms by physical treatments such as adjustments, nutrition, and herbal remedies. Most of these reversals of emotional/mental symptoms took place without any active emotional or mental participation by the patient. The body treatments alone healed both their emotional and mental problems.

This is not to take away from emotional/mental approaches to healing. They are equally important if the CAUSE of their symptom/problem is emotional or mental. In my practice I found that more mental/emotional symptoms were caused by physical body malfunctions than mental/emotional problems were causing physical problems. A therapist could certainly have clients with mental/emotional problems causing physical symptoms like headaches, back pain, or even worse.

Let's talk about Cause for a moment, big C. If something is wrong with you as defined by your own opinion, then by definition it has to have a CAUSE. But the problem you describe is usually a symptom. Symptoms are what you describe as wrong with you. "I have a headache." "I'm depressed." "I can't concentrate." These sound like they could be a physical, emotional, or mental problem, but actually they are still only symptoms. Please pay attention to the next paragraph.

Every symptom has a CAUSE. And here is an important key. Not all symptoms are caused directly from where they show up. A true CAUSE can easily create a symptom far from the symptom's location, and even in a different system.

Let me explain. Let's call the physical, emotional, and mental aspects of your body "locations." You have a physical location (body), an emotional location (emotions), and a mental location (thinking).

The symptom can affect one or more of these three locations. It has to reflect in your body somewhere. You feel a pain in your knee, your shoulder aches, you have a sharp headache. However, this is still only the location of the symptom. If you are emotionally depressed, you believe it is something wrong with your emotions. If your mind is driving a high anxiety state, your racing thoughts make you feel like you have a mental problem.

Here is an important understanding. It is relatively easy to know where a symptom is affecting you. Your body hurts somewhere, your emotions are upset or out of balance. Your mind is not thinking or acting correctly in the way you think it should.

What's more difficult is to determine a CAUSE for the location where you are experiencing the symptoms. Some problems seem very typical, let's say your knee hurts. It has to be something wrong with your knee, right? This could be, but not necessarily.

An ankle or hip problem often causes knee pain. It could be a growth behind the knee. It could be a muscle that is contracting because you are tense about an upcoming job interview next week. You might have an emotional fear of running into someone at work so making your knee hurt means you don't have to attend an event where this person will be.

Again, let's keep things simple. Let's say that your knee hurts, so you go to a knee doctor. S/he does something to your knee, and it feels better; end of symptom. So far this seems physical and so be it, but what if it comes back? Was it really treated at the level of the cause? Or was the symptom being treated on a symptomatic level?

"Fixing a symptom" versus "treating the cause" are two different procedures entirely. For example, you could have a red light blinking in the dashboard of your car. That's a symptom telling you something is wrong with your engine. You could easily make that symptom go away by cutting the wire to the light, thus no more blinking light. Symptom gone!

Clearly however, this is not a good strategy as there was likely a deeper cause to the blinking red light. Just making the blinking red light stop is not going to get to the Cause of the engine problem. This would be similar to taking an aspirin to stop a headache. The headache is your blinking red light. Just turning off the pain doesn't help you understand the cause of your headache.

Taking an aspirin to make a headache go away defines "treating a symptom." If you get a headache once a year, no big deal. If you get a headache every day, that's different. If you get really severe headaches, this is different still. You need to be willing to explore CAUSES outside the box when dealing with moderate to difficult problems.

Simple solutions to common problems can be easily identified. However, nothing in the body is so 100% true that some other factor couldn't change things. For example, headaches can be caused by many different sources. Some obvious possibilities are a bad diet, lack of sleep, being overworked and under paid, family or social stress, etc.

The point is that every symptom has a Cause. Your symptom may be perceived in a physical, emotional, or mental location within your body. However, the source of the CAUSE may come from a different location than the symptom:

Chapter 7: Introducing Your Personal World

1. A Physical CAUSE can create, manifest, or develop an Emotional or Mental location symptom.
2. An Emotional CAUSE can create, manifest, or develop a Physical or Mental location symptom.
3. A Mental CAUSE can create, manifest, or develop a Physical or Emotional location symptom.

A simple way of explaining a physical CAUSE is when a damaged wire goes to a speaker, the sound will not come through clearly as expected. If you don't water a plant, the leaves will start to whither and fall off. If your body is missing nutrition, hormonal support or you are simply physically over-tired, your emotions or mind will not function as clearly as expected. A simple lack of B-12 can cause "depression-like" symptoms. Which means to me that it causes depression.

As an experienced SELF-Parenting practitioner, you will need to be open to a wide spectrum of information if you encounter a personal symptom that is difficult and requires deeper levels of healing. Sometimes an obvious solution does not fix what appears to be an obvious problem.

Perhaps you've tried a multitude of emotional/mental approaches to solve a problem. but if it's caused by a physical cause, you need a physical remedy. Suffice to say that your body's hardware is super important. It is the basis of your emotional and mental well-being, so take care of your body to the best of your ability.

In my experience physical CAUSES can create more emotional and mental SYMPTOMS than are understood by the public. Professionals can miss these causes as well. For example, let's say you went to a psychologist so solve a headache problem. What kind of solution would s/he be looking to implement? Based on their training it would be an emotional or mental solution. Perhaps you went there specifically because "regular doctors" told you your problems were "in your head." What most "regular doctors" don't know is that spinal problems in the neck are by far the major cause of severe headaches.

Emotional or Mental symptoms created by physical causes can be deeper and harder to locate until you know how to start looking for them. Once you become aware of the many potential physical causes, you will find they are everywhere. Many of the physical CAUSES for emotional and mental symptoms can be missed by professionals who only know to look in their area of specialty. If your problem is not caused by their area of concern, basically they dismiss you as a nut case.

Perhaps the most prevalent type of physical cause for a plethora of body, emotional, and mental symptoms is eating refined sugar and flour. These two substances can give your body every physical, emotional, and mental symptom what man can name.

For example, if you experience severe emotional depression, you'll never know if sugar or flour is the root cause until you stop eating sugar and flour on a daily basis. If you do and in three days you are not depressed anymore, what does this tell you? Taking pills, exercise, and meditation are other methods of treating depression symptoms yet may not provide lasting relief until you stop eating sugar and flour.

Another point I've noticed is that people with super strong bodies are often able to excel in amazing emotional and mental pursuits with seemingly little effort without ever recognizing how important their amazing body was to their success. Mentally, they think of themselves as the same as everyone else. They don't realize that everything is easier for them because they were gifted with a stronger, more able neurological foundation.

Chapter 7: Introducing Your Personal World

Because their "feelings symptoms" may appear as emotional or mental, they often seek an emotional or mental solution. Suppose at some point they start feeling depressed. Even though their run-down body is the cause, they don't consider this possibility, because their body is still physically strong.

People who over-exercise can build up stress that affects them emotionally/mentally. Their solution? More exercise because that's what made them feel better in the past. They push themselves harder as an Inner Parent and continue to run their strong and excellent body at maximum performance to their own detriment.

At some point, which eventually does occur, their body becomes run down from the stress. These are also the same people that have a heart attack after having received a complete bill of health from their latest doctor exam. So, a word to the wise, take care of your body.

Just to summarize, your common symptoms, "I have a headache," "I'm depressed," or "I can't concentrate," may seem physical, emotional, or mental on the surface, but in reality, they could be Caused by any of the three. The most ignored when it counts the most in my personal experience, are the physical causes that create emotional and mental symptoms. And I'm the guy who came up with Self-Parenting.

Chapter 8:
Let's Talk About Emotional

Chapter 8: Let's Talk About Emotional

The second aspect of your Personal World is defined as your emotional self. For the SELF-Parenting practitioner, you know this as your Inner Child. Let's speak briefly to the reader who might not yet be familiar with the concept of their "Inner Child." In SELF-Parenting we assign all the aspects of our emotional side to the inner voice we call the Inner Child.

Emotions are very influential in your Personal world. People typically have no true control when it comes to balancing their emotions over their "reasoning". Advertisers know that if they can get to a person's emotions, they can move them to do whatever they want them to do.

However, the real goal for us as human beings is to learn to consciously participate in a 50-50 relationship with the emotions of our Inner Child. Each of us has this emotional part of us, whether we admit to this or not.

Ideally the relationship with our emotions works in the same way as a seesaw in a children's playground. As you may have experienced, when operating a seesaw there needs to be an equal sized partner on the other side for the seesaw to work correctly. Think of your body as providing the physical seesaw structure for your emotions and mind. Your emotions as the Inner Child are on one side, and your mind as the Inner Parent takes the other seat on the seesaw.

From the perspective of the seesaw, your emotions get jurisdiction and control over its half of your seesaw. Your mind is assigned the other half. Your emotions provide the desire which acts as the fuel to energize your seesaw. The logic and planning from your mental side uses the emotional desires and energies of your Inner Child to accomplish your mutual needs and desires. It behooves both participants on your SELF-Parenting seesaw to cooperate by contributing their individual strengths to achieve a mutual win/win result.

You can't control your emotions if they don't want to be controlled. They are on the other side of the seesaw. You can impact and influence your emotions from your side, but not directly control them. This is especially true during situations of severe duress, traumatic injuries, or extreme weather events, etc.

During high impact events like this you are not even invited to participate as the Inner Parent until the immediate emergency is settled down. Even technically if there isn't an "emergency" happening, your emotions can easily act "as if" there is a crisis going on.

Your emotional feelings are only half of your SELF-Parenting relationship. Your Inner Child needs the Mental as much as your Inner Parent needs the Emotional. It's nice when a person can enjoy a positive working relationship between his/her emotions and mind, especially as occurs when practicing SELF-Parenting. This is based on assumption that at some point in your life you will be introduced to each other and begin the cooperative sessions that improve your lives together.

It's important for you to recognize the difference between your Inner Parent (not the emotions), and who you are as the Inner Child (not the thinking). Simply by being born, it's as if you signed a 50/50 contract to live the rest of your life together. This is the true "until death do us part" relationship.

Emotional reactions have been shown to be a complex interaction involving both the body and mind. Emotions produce chemical reactions in the brain and cells. The body responds to emotions with electrical and magnetic nerve signals. Your

Chapter 8: Let's Talk About Emotional

emotional side varies on a scale, from high to low, glad to sad, love to hate, etc.

A "good" emotion and a "bad" emotion are still emotions. Various philosophies have various scales based on various measurements. If you do a web search for Images for Emotional Scales, you will have many to choose from. Even so, both the emotions and the mind rely on the physical structure of the body and require a healthy body for optimum function.

If your Inner Child is resisting emotionally what the Inner Parent wants to do mentally, it's going to be very difficult for you to accomplish whatever you are trying to do. The Inner Child likes to resist passively, by not providing energy. It also has powerful abilities to "act out" in certain situations.

This may seem paradoxical, but its typically harder for you to know and diagnose the blockages and miscommunication between your inner selves than any stranger standing on the street. Let me explain.

One reason is because you, as the Inner Parent, ignore the deeper levels of your emotional side. You're stuck inside your inner conversations and you have gotten used to being stuck. Someone who is not personally involved with you could potentially take five seconds to figure out what's blocking the interaction between your Inner Child and Inner Parent. You on the other hand, are so used to blocking yourself that you can't even see it.

Use what you learn from your emotional side to guide your inner relationship towards a win/win experience. If nothing else, your Inner Child wants to be happy and your Inner Parent wants to feel positive. If your Inner Child is not happy or your Inner Parent is not feeling positive, this can be an excellent "blinking red light" to signal this is a good time to start paying attention to your inner dialogue.

A major aspect of your Personal World is to allocate the energy created between your body, emotions, and mind for your own personal purposes as opposed to the vast amounts of energy required to maintain your outer relationships.

As you will see in the next few chapters, the main focus of our lives typically take place in our outer Relational World which is not your Personal World. It takes lots of outer energy to keep our many outer relationship seesaws energized, balanced, and working properly. This means the personal relationship between our internal emotions and mind can become neglected if we are not careful.

Some people put all their energy into their Personal World. Some people put all their energy into their Relational World. Some people put all their energy into their Financial World.

Putting all your energy into any one world exclusively can be a superficial strategy to achieve what looks like success. However, this has consequences for the other two worlds if you neglect to distribute energy in a balanced way. If you rely too much on one world for your happiness and subsequently lose the assets associated with this world, then you can feel very distraught indeed.

For example, if you put all your energy into your Relational World, and then lose all your friends, you are going to be very unhappy. If you are a millionaire and lose all your money, you are going to be very unhappy. Ideal logic suggests distributing an equal amount of energy into each of the three worlds which is certainly a goal you can strive to achieve.

WHO IS YOUR INNER CHILD?

Your Inner Child is a complete and distinctly separate self from your Inner Parent. Your Inner Child is the bouncy, bubbly, and happy side of you. It represents your feelings, emotions, and reactions to the world. Your Inner Child is the voice that represents your body when asking for the fulfillment of a physical need or desire.

This voice can be quite insistent and loud. Demands such as, "I'm hungry," "I'm tired," "I'm bored," "This is ridiculous," "I don't want to go to work." "I don't feel well," "I want..." can often be heard sounding off within you.

The same characteristics you had as an outer child from birth to age seven are the same characteristics your Inner Child has today. The dreams and adventures you once desired are those of your Inner Child today. Whatever your chronological age, your emotional side still has a sweet, innocent, loving Inner Child within you.

It's very important to understand that your Inner Child is a separate voice within your mind. There will never be a time when your Inner Child voice merges with your Inner Parent. During meditation it's possible for both inner voices to quieten, or even stop conversing for a period of time. But the two sides will never merge into one.

Just like you are separate from your outer parents, your Inner Child is its own distinct self. Know that, just like an outer child, your Inner Child, can have positive or negative aspects. The positive side is felt as ENTHUSIASM! Don't you see every young child you know running here and there, never stopping; climbing everything, picking up anything, and constantly pushing buttons on phones, televisions, and videos?

This trait is VERY IMPORTANT because this enthusiasm and excitement is what floods both inner selves with the well-being and happiness that are essential qualities of happy living. If you enjoyed these feelings as a child but now they feel like a distant memory, when you embrace and support your Inner Child these feelings will come pouring back into your life.

When things are going well having fun while experiencing life is the main role of your Inner Child. She/he can find joy and fulfillment in the simplest pleasures. The Inner Child loves playing games and experiencing new adventures along with learning and practicing new skills in any area of its interests.

Regardless of your gender, your Inner Child can be male or female. This is something I did not normally discuss when teaching in the early days. I simply let each person experience their Inner Child as whichever gender felt natural to them without making a fuss over it either way.

As society has evolved these questions of gender identity have come more to the fore. It is the gender your Inner Child feels which represents the dynamic for those with conflicting perceptions based on their biological gender. (The Inner Parent can also have a gender that differs from physical biology.)

I never considered that it was necessary to "give the Inner Child a name," although many early SELF-Parenting Practitioners did this as other psychologists had made a point of this idea with "inner child" work. If your Inner Child indicates a desire to be called by a certain name, then certainly you would honor that request, just like you would for any friend.

I would be careful of arbitrarily giving your Inner Child. a name. It may not like the name it was called as a child, even if it's familiar. If your Inner Child didn't like the name you chose,

I'm sure you'd hear about it quickly enough if you are paying attention. It's a simple question to ask your Inner Child if it has a name it prefers to be called. It goes like this, "Inner Child do you have a name you'd like to be called?"

Children love to learn. It's what they do. So an important role for your Inner Parent is to provide your Inner Child with new learning opportunities. Know that you will often be required to be the teacher of your Inner Child. He or she is usually willing to learn, explore, or do just about anything the Inner Parent wants within reason.

Your Inner Child wants to please you (the Inner Parent). But just like teaching an outer child to swim, if you toss it in the deep end of the pool on its first lesson this might not go well. The better approach is to begin in the shallow end and let your Inner Child learn to enjoy the feeling of getting wet.

Any new teaching or experience should be approached using a gradient from simple to complex. Your Inner Child can learn any advanced or complicated topic that is presented with logical steps starting from simple to complex. This is especially true when the Inner Child has a strong desire to learn the subject or topic.

Start with basic introductory theory and build step-by-step just like any course of knowledge. If you get a strong sense of resistance from your Inner Child for any activity, you would certainly dialog and ask your Inner Child about this resistance during your SELF-Parenting sessions.

Here is something I learned very early in my studies which has helped me tremendously when reading or studying. When learning a new topic or discipline, never go past a word you do not understand. If you read a word you don't understand, your

Inner Parent needs to look it up and understand what it means. This is true for both inner selves but is particularly important for your Inner Child when beginning any new topic of study.

Every system of study potentially has its own terminology and complicated procedures to learn. This is why it's a system of study. Electricians, musicians, and mathematicians all have complicated words or unique usage of an otherwise common word. Scientists, baseball players, and dinosaur experts all have to learn crazy words that no one else has to bother with.

Another crucial factor for learning any new activity is your Inner Child's innate desire. If your Inner Parent is the one that wants to achieve some practice or goal, and the Inner Child has zero interest, it's going to be a long series of trials before you eventually give up. If your Inner Child is fascinated and strongly eager for some project or idea, seize that opportunity as an Inner Parent to look into it. As your regular SELF-Parenting sessions grow and deepen you will naturally explore various scenarios that arise.

It's important for the Inner Parent to understand that the Inner Child is the owner of the feelings. You (the Inner Parent) cannot experience an emotion unless first generated by the Inner Child. All the genuine emotions that come from "you" are actually coming from your Inner Child. The Inner Parent may act on the information provided by the emotions, but it is your Inner Child that originally feels them.

The most important aspect to understand is that your Inner Child is as unique and individual a personality like any other outer child. Outer parents know that each child they have is different and unique in ways only they can be. It's the same for your Inner Child. You only get one Inner Child so accept him/her as s/he is.

Chapter 8: Let's Talk About Emotional

This is easier to understand in the outer world, because an outer child is actually a separate person. When this is an internal aspect of your mind, the separation is trickier to distinguish. The SELF-Parenting Program provides a half hour session protocol called the 23 Tips. When you follow this practice, you learn how to separate the personalities of the two selves. By asking questions in this manner you will soon learn the combination of traits and desires that make up your Inner Child. The role of the Inner Parent is to embrace and honor the unique potential and traits of his/her Inner Child.

Through your daily SELF-Parenting sessions, you will become more knowledgeable and intimate with your Inner Child than ever before possible. This precious self is your companion for life. Not only this, but your Inner Child can also be your most ferocious protector if the need arises. When the relationship between you is strong and honest nobody is on your side more than your Inner Child.

If your outer parenting was hostile or negative, this means you will have more of an uphill battle to turn this pattern around within your own Inner Conversations. To correct problems of this nature the Inner Child must be made to feel safe again. The responsibility to change a negative Inner Child lies directly with the Inner Parent. Devoting thirty minutes a day to the SELF-Parenting Exercises provides your Inner Parent the time necessary to love and nurture your Inner Child so that its voice can once again be heard without negative judgments.

The key to positive SELF-Parenting within your mind is for you, as the Inner Parent, to take the initiative and become a receiver for the voice of the Inner Child. Your SELF-Parenting practice along with the Self-Parenting Modules initiate the beginning strides towards developing a conscious relationship with your Inner Child.

As your practice time grows, your ability to listen will continue to deepen and become more intimate. To regain the energy and enthusiasm for living you had as a child, you will learn to rely more and more on this inner self within you.

As your day-to-day experience with your SELF-Parenting grows, there's a technique taught the Intermediate practitioners. The basic idea is when faced with decisions that could go one way or the other, defer to the choice of your Inner Child. Letting your Inner Child lead or decide what both selves should do is an excellent strategy for this adventure called life.

I am not talking about going directly against the needs of the Inner Parent. This is more for when you have a choice of options for a meal, or a vacation, or a new car. Typically, your Inner Child will be happier and feel more like a true partner in your life when it's choice is accepted or approved for a life decision. Doing what your Inner Child wants is an easy way to move your life forward even if the Inner Parent is reluctant.

As far as specific techniques and dynamics to work with your Inner Child during your SELF-Parenting sessions, this is best left to the progression of the SELF-Parenting Modules. Each module deepens your SELF-Parenting interaction. Remember that growth in SELF-Parenting is mostly about the Inner Parent. The Inner Child will always do well if treated correctly and fairly by the Inner Parent. So much of the day-to-day happiness of the Inner Child is reflected by how well your Inner Parent does its job.

Chapter 9:
Let's Talk About Mental

Chapter 9: Let's Talk About Mental

Your "Mind":

The "mind" is typically where most people place the thinking and planning a person does to live his/her life. This is generally described as "thinking" thoughts. In the SELF-Parenting Program, we see "the mind" as a set of ongoing "inner conversations" between your Inner Parent and Inner Child. This includes both the emotions of the Inner Child as well as the thoughts of the Inner Parent as they engage in constant interactive communication with each other.

Most of us consider our thinking as the daily planning and navigation of our ongoing life activities. We have a set of daily habits that we've evolved so far in our life. When we mentally notice some vague thought that registers discomfort we start thinking of some action or solution that might help. This is what normal people do and we are all normal aren't we?

Humanity has created a multitude of mental philosophies, religions, and political ideologies from the beginning of time. Many of them isolate thoughts and thinking based on the perspective of the Inner Parent alone. There are so many systems for "positive mental thinking" that there is no way to describe them all. Yet if a mental system becomes too one-sided, it can leave out the emotions completely.

There are times when your mental side, the pattern you are thinking on a day-to-day basis, must change. As an advanced SELF-Parenting practitioner, I am going to suggest you explore the mental system that has helped me the most in my life outside of the context of SELF-Parenting. This aspect of training for the Inner Parent has always been part of my intermediate and advanced consultations. The following system is truly designed for the Inner Parent to "up its game" and take responsibility in matters of mental thinking.

There's a good chance you've heard a saying that goes something like, "Only you can make yourself upset." There have many expressions communicating this idea from ancient times to the present day. So much so that this concept has practically become a cliché. However, if you can develop the skills of your Inner Parent, you will find that it truly is so.

The basic premise is that no one or nothing can make you upset unless you allow it. This seems to go against the reality of life for most people. If something bad happens to you, it only seems natural that this terrible event or experience will make your mind upset. The idea that a person could be happy despite the variety of negative events that can happen in a single day, is almost impossible to believe.

We typically run into this idea that "our mental thinking creates our reality" at a time when experiencing some form of extreme unhappiness. We are seeking some way to make a difficult outer world problem go away. We strongly experience and want to eliminate our negative thoughts/feelings. As we take a closer look at the source of our unhappiness, at some point we come across this concept that we are creating our own unhappiness by the way we are thinking.

For many people, the first time this idea entered the mainstream of human awareness AND was accompanied by realistic tools that actually worked, was in the book I'm going to recommend next. This was certainly not the first time this idea was ever presented. Philosophers and teachers from all ages and cultures have made this point that we create our own reality.

For me the first time this concept was clearly explained along with a set of practical mental tools to achieve this objective was described in the book written by Ken Keyes, Jr, called *The Handbook to Higher Consciousness*.

Chapter 9: Let's Talk About Mental

There is no way to praise this book enough. Ken's book provides major mental insights that represent a mental breakthrough still today. The basic premise of Ken's book is as follows. We mentally make ourselves upset if we have an "addictive demand." This is defined as a mental thought or belief that something should be different than what life is giving us.

The basic goal of the system is to recognize addictive demands when experiencing them and then change them to a preference. If you prefer that something be different than the way it is, you won't get upset. If you addictively demand that something be different than the way it is, you will make yourself upset.

He called his methods the Living Love System. There are more details to this of course, but I am keeping it simple until you get your own copy of his book and can study this from the source.

Addictive demands have many forms and occur as thoughts on either side of our inner conversations. Some simple examples are as follows. "They should not say that…" "That noise is too loud…" "This soup is too cold…" "I hate my job/boss…" Basically, any experience given to you by life that you are unwilling to accept, has the potential to be an addictive demand.

Because you do not like something that life has presented, you make yourself upset over the issue. You want it to stop or change, or make it go away somehow. Yet for whatever reason, this is not possible. Therefore, you continue to experience this "addictive demand" that you not be bothered by this person, place, or event that is bothering you. It could be anything from minor to major in your life. Whatever it is, you are upset about it. It could be something you want or something you don't want.

From the perspective of changing this specific pattern, I put this on the Inner Parent's side of the seesaw. If the Inner Child is upset about something that's a different situation and is handled in a different way per SELF-Parenting protocols. But when it's the Inner Parent (mind) who has the addictive demand, the Inner Child can be completely out of the loop.

Addictive demands apply most clearly when the Inner Parent is unhappy. This can occur in many areas of life. There can be so many ways that life doesn't cooperate with what you want to do. Not only is a bus late, but it never comes. A promise someone made to you in person is broken without warning. Something you've worked hard for never takes place. A goal that you did achieve created a totally different result than you expected. Your tire is flat, your neighbor is too loud, or a heavy jar fell on your foot. You can accept these events as a reality in your life, or you can make yourself upset about them until the end of time.

When your Inner Parent has an addictive demand regarding some situation, the problem is with the Inner Parent. Your Inner Child is not equipped to deal with this correctly. This could be compared to a similar situation in an outer family relationship.

If one or both of the "outer parents" are unhappy about some adult issue, this can be very upsetting for the child. However, there is not much the child in the family can do to help the outer parent(s). It is a situation only the adult(s) can handle.

The goal of Ken's system is for your Inner Parent to turn any and every "addictive demand" into a "preference." If you allow the addictive demand to continue, you will continue to make yourself upset. If you can turn your "addictive demand" into a "preference," this situation will no longer make you upset. At first it takes a lot of courage and practice to notice and admit to

Chapter 9: Let's Talk About Mental

these addictive demands. But like any skill, the more you practice the better you will become.

As Ken points out so well, no one can create a life where s/he gets exactly what they want all the time. As he said many times, "in life you win some and you lose some." Even the richest, most handsome/beautiful, most famous/powerful person in the world is not able to create a life where they will always get everything they want. Life has an unerring way of presenting you with random events that can trigger an "addictive demand" for things not to be this way.

It is however, completely within your ability to live life on a preferential basis. This will determine the amount of happiness you experience playing the game called life. The more you change addictive demands to preferences, the more internal joy and happiness you will experience.

Let's say you are craving a specific brand of chocolate ice cream but none is available. If you truly addictively demand this chocolate ice cream, you could drive to three different stores and make yourself more upset at each store if it's not available. No other flavor of ice cream will satisfy you.

Or, you can "prefer" to have this exact same brand of ice cream, but if it turns out not to be available despite your best efforts, you will not make yourself upset. After all it was just a preference, ultimately you could take it or leave it.

Maybe you can be just as happy with one of the 30 other flavors from which to choose. Maybe you won't eat ice cream at all and have some cake instead. The point is that changing any addictive demand to a preference is the ultimate key to achieving and keeping a happy state of mind.

Working on "addictive demands" takes place outside the realm of SELF-Parenting. This is true "Inner Parent work." When your Inner Parent studies and applies the Living Love system, you can clear up all kinds of mental problems/issues, that SELF-Parenting just isn't designed to fix.

So many times, in my life when I was experiencing a major upset about something. I would pick up **The Handbook to Higher Consciousness**, open it to any page, and within three sentences have the exact reason I was making myself so angry, or hurt, or whatever it was I was doing to myself at the time.

Quite simply, I, as the Inner Parent, was addictively demanding a person, an event, or a situation be other than it actually was. Once I changed my addictive demand to a preference, the mental/emotional disturbance would miraculously pass.

Note that it is possible to have a mental issue create what feels like a negative emotion, but it's actually negative thinking on the part of the Inner Parent. An example might be that you as the Inner Parent don't like the clothes your date is wearing. Because of this, you create a mood or dislike that feels like a negative "emotion" even though it is really based on an Inner Parent judgment.

There are many nuances on this idea which you will recognize for yourself when you get to this stage in your SELF-Parenting growth. Suffice to say that reading Ken's book will give you much more detail and understanding about the concept of "addictive demands." You need to study, learn, and apply the methods in his book for your continued growth as an Inner Parent. Until you can live a life mostly free of addictive demands, you will still be susceptible to the various ways that life can irritate you.

Unfortunately, the Living Love System as an outer school where you could go to learn these things has disappeared. When Ken died, he left no heirs to his teachings. However, his book is very well written and explains everything you need to know to work with the system. This is not something you do inside your SELF-Parenting sessions. This is study your Inner Parent takes on its own and there will be much that needs to be done.

You start by getting familiar with what he calls the 12 Pathways. These are basically 12 sentences that you read to yourself to help rewire your thought patterns and to help you learn to recognize your addictive demands. Making a copy, keeping them with you, and reading them when you are upset is also very helpful.

Memorizing the 12 Pathways brings them even deeper into your mental programming. This was a mandatory step before taking any of his trainings and is highly recommended. He also suggests four additional "Living Love Methods" that can be applied at various times in various situations as you need them.

In my opinion it is impossible to get to the higher levels of SELF-Parenting consciousness, without going through the Inner Parent process of digging out your addictive demands using Ken's work. And there could be many paths to reaching this understanding. Ken's book is not the only way to learn these ideas.

Buddhist thought is very aligned with this concept. Various teachers who achieved this internal state have taught their own methods or ways. Every major religious or philosophical teaching has some version of this idea in its teaching. It's just that Ken's book tells it for the first time in a modern way that is truly usable. It's not just something he tells us to do. He teaches the methods to achieve this worthy goal. We are all very lucky to have this resource. Fortunately, his book is still available on Amazon.

On a personal note, in his later years Ken became a personal friend of mine. He read SELF-Parenting during the early 90's and truly got the message which was of great comfort to me. He invited me up to Coos Bay, Oregon to present at his college. He visited me in Malibu to have lunch.

His final book was basically an ode to SELF-Parenting, which could have been good for me, but unfortunately, he passed soon after its publication. As a longtime fan of Ken since 1972, it was amazing to me that my most respected guru took on and converted to the teachings of his devoted student without any direct intervention on my part.

WHO IS YOUR INNER PARENT?

From the perspective of your mind and thinking in general, your Inner Parent represents the main functionality of your mental side. Anything you can do to become a better Inner Parent will strengthen your skill set as the Inner Parent.

This might be a good time to also honor Thomas Gordon, the author who first presented *P.E.T. Parent Effectiveness Training* to the world. As mentioned earlier, his book was instrumental for the wisdom and insights which I found very helpful to create and develop the SELF-Parenting Program. A side note of interest is that he was based in Pasadena, CA, which was where I was also living when I discovered his work.

What's most amazing about his discoveries is that his main principles established for the "parenting role" can also be directly applied to the leadership role in other areas. For example, his next book was *T.E.T: Teacher Effectiveness Training*. Here

Chapter 9: Let's Talk About Mental

he described the Teacher/Student relationship and defined the essential roles/rules that applied for each Copartner. Note that the Teacher role is very similar to the Parent role

Then he went straight for the business market with ***L.E.T: Leadership Effectiveness Training.*** Here he pointed out that the ideal Boss is very similar in principle to the ideal Parent or Teacher. I read and studied them all. He simply restructured the basic principles of positive parenting but fit them into the teaching and leadership relationships.

The genius of Thomas Gordon's was to show how the leadership purpose in any relationship could be upgraded to a cooperative win/win result. This was to replace the "do what I say and do it now" mentality which was the prevailing logic of the parenting, teaching, or leadership roles prior to his writings.

The fact that he utilized his basic relationship principles for each of these outer disciplines (parenting, teaching, business) reflects the genius of his approach. Applying his outer parenting guidelines to the Inner Parent made it incredibly easy for me to establish safe guidelines for the role of the Inner Parent.

As you might be aware, reading ***P.E.T.*** is also Step 7 of the Ten Steps to Intermediate SELF-Parenting. There is no way to calculate how influential his ideas and genius became as they spread around the world. To take this even one step deeper, the ultimate genius of the SELF-Parenting Program is that when you become an excellent Inner Parent to your Inner Child, you also will excel at outer parenting, teaching, or leading a company. It's the only way you know how to be and your children, students, or employees will be the beneficiaries.

To sum up the Mental side of life from the SELF-Parenting point of view we can say two things. Learn to become a better Inner

Parent and take care of your addictive demands by upgrading them to preferences. After this you are free to explore mental topics however you like. It's your life after all and it's a big world out there.

Next, we are going to move from the topic of your Personal World, where you are the master of your domain, and step into your "Relational World" where many of us spend the majority of our time. In this world you are no longer in complete control as you will soon discover but may already intuitively understand.

Chapter 10:

Your "Relational World" Interacting with Outer People

Chapter 10: Your "Relational World" Interacting with Outer People

From the perspective of the individual, each person resides within three intersecting worlds of a Personal, Relational and Financial nature. At the time of this writing, we dwell in an ocean of approximately 7.8 billion other people, each having his/her own three worlds for which s/he is responsible. The unique instance of our "personal world" is defined by our body, emotions and mind. No other person is part of this equation. However, this view represents an abstraction.

If we take the perspective of humanity as a species, it's more accurate to suggest that each person is simply one drop of water flowing in a vast ocean of relationships with other people. It's like we are only one bee in a hive of bees. We are one gorilla in a pack of gorillas. Even as we first become aware of who we are as a human, it is only within a group of relationships. If other people weren't taking care of us, we would never have survived to know we had a Personal World in the first place.

The simple fact is we begin our human experience in relationships with other humans. This is where the definition of the "outer" world begins. Once you are interacting with other humans, you transfer from your Personal World to firmly enter your Relational World. You are now using your body, emotions and mind to interact with another person's body, emotions and mind. Your Personal World becomes secondary to this larger "Relational World."

Relationships involve interacting with other people which is self-evident. Yet most people don't typically separate the difference between their Personal and Relational Worlds. For many people their life is simply a set of worldly experiences jumbled up with other people as if piled into a big washing machine and swirled around at a frantic pace. For them there is simply too much action going on for them to easily separate their body/feelings/thoughts from all the relational activity.

Yet, these 2 areas of life (worlds) Personal and Relational, operate by different rules. Starting now, you will be able to consciously distinguish between these two worlds. This will help your two inner selves to create more successful relationship experiences to the best of your ability and skill level.

Your first dawn of awareness occurs as a new member joining this "Relational World." Ideally your birth was fortunate enough to have 2 parents that brought you up in a loving, caring home environment. If so, this means right away you began life as one half of not one but two outer relationships. The relationship between your 2 outer parents literally created "your relational world." Being born automagically placed you on your half of both a Mother/Child and Father/Child relationship seesaw (assuming the ideal).

If you had brothers or sisters, you also became one-half of one or more Sibling/Sibling relationship(s). If your parents had brothers or sisters that lived nearby this means you were automatically enrolled in Aunt or Uncle relationships. The parents of your parents could still be alive which places you inevitably as one half of a Grandparent/Grandchild relationship. Every living person has a unique Relational World based on his/her family constellation of outer relationships.

Simply growing up creates your learning about relationships in the outer world before you have any control or knowledge of what's going on. The patterns in these relationships internalize naturally to become part of your experience and knowledge as to how relationships work. By default, your experiences growing up in your outer family become the foundation for your understanding of how outer relationships work. This is true in

Chapter 10: Your "Relational World" Interacting with Outer People

exactly the same way that how you were parented became your SELF-Parenting style. It's the same process in a larger setting. Your life experiences provide the programming of your human brain.

Because you've never experienced anything different and did not know any better, you just assumed that the way things were/are in your family, are the way things are for all families. If some of your experiences growing up were let's say, "outside the norm," it may take you many years to discover that the way you were brought up might not reflect how most people experienced growing up.

Let's assume your early family life was "normal" within your culture and country. During your school years you'll commonly enter the training program for your next circle of Social Relationships. This is your education going to school, growing up as a student, learning social norms, language, and math skills. This continues as you move through your middle and high school years interacting with a wider range of fellow students and teachers.

As time passes you gradually experience a wider range of relationships in the form of expanded family members, neighbors, outside caretakers, doctors, people who work in stores, etc. At some point, you may enter the world of Work Relationships to earn money and begin to create and establish a life more tuned to your individual desires and personality.

All these experiences take place within your Relational World. Funnily enough, it is unlikely that at any time during this roughly 18-24-year period, anyone will specifically and clearly teach you how relationships work. You simply absorb what happens to you in relationships through your basic life experiences. You will internalize your own working model of how relationships work based on the combination of the various interactions you encounter in this "real world" along with the fictionalized world of TV and movies within your culture.

Combine this with the fact that growing up we are generally not exposed to much "inner work." Nor are we typically encouraged to develop our body, emotions and minds without a lot of interference from outside people and authority figures. It's no wonder we arrive at adulthood without a clear distinction between our Personal and Relational worlds nor any true understanding in reality of how relationships work.

To summarize this introduction, your Relational World involves all the people and interactions you've experienced with others growing up on a daily basis. Your parents, your siblings, your schools, your neighborhood, your country and whatever other experiences you've had with other people all contribute to your understanding of your relational world.

In general, everybody has relationships. What's different for you, is that your birth created a unique instance of a human life. YOUR relationship world is a version and combination of people and relationships that exist solely because of you.

The specific relationships you've experienced, the ones that impacted you, are called your Personal Relationships because they are the ones you personally experienced. You've learned how relationships work based on the totality of various experiences you encountered growing up.

Your interactions as a family member provide your first relational training. They taught you how relationships work at least within your family. Next, schooling taught you the social relationship norms for your particular culture. If you were lucky

Chapter 10: Your "Relational World" Interacting with Outer People

you were able to learn and experience a wider variety of cultural relationships as you matured.

For all the estimated 7.8 billion people living on this planet, each one has a unique version of a "Personal Relationship Word." However, grouping relationships from a generic perspective, they can be assigned to three major types with a total of 12 categories.

The three major types of human relationships are:

- Family Relationships
- Social Relationships
- Work Relationships

The Family type of relationships includes 5 categories:

- Parent/Child (you can be a parent or a child)
- Sibling/Sibling (you as a sibling)
- Grandparent/Grandchild (you can be either)
- Other Kin (lots of types)
- Adult Child/Aging Parent (you as either role)

The Social type of relationships includes 5 categories:

- Friend/Friend relationships (you as a friend)
- Boyfriend/Girlfriend relationships (you as either)
- Husband/Wife relationships (you as either)
- In-Law/In-Law relationships (you as either)
- Neighbor/Neighbor relationships (you as either)

The Work type of relationships includes 2 basic categories:

- Boss/Employee relationships (you as either)
- Coworker/Coworker relationships (you as a coworker)

The next chapter will look at the specific anatomy of how a single relationship works. Each relationship in the 12 categories has three parts that operate in essentially the same way. There is a core functionality with a set way to understand relationships in a balanced and unbiased manner.

Learning this model provides the foundational core that will clarify your understanding of all your personal outer relationships. Once you understand how any relationship is designed to work, you can then pick out the details and purpose that makes each relationship category successful at achieving the needs of both copartners.

Chapter 11:

A Brief Outline of How Relationships Work

Chapter 11: A Brief Outline of How Relationships Work

Learning how relationships work can seem like a vast impossibility. Certainly, that's how it's presented in academic and social teachings. But it's not complicated once you define the three parts of any relationship and realize how similarly they all function. In fact, it's so simple even an eight-year-old can understand it. Just imagine a seesaw in a children's playground. If you know how a seesaw works, the rest is easy.

Once you adopt this easy-to-learn relationship model, you can place each of the various people and situations from your entire life into the model. You can then use the model to assess how closely the relationships you experienced compare to what most people call "normal."

You can also do this with the relationships you read about in books, see on TV, or watch in movies that you like. This is truly a universal system for understanding how relationships work. Anyone of any age can place his/her or any other person's (fact or fiction) relationships into the seesaw model to describe and discuss specific details concerning that relationship.

The HRW seesaw model defines a relationship as having three parts. When a relationship follows the ideal model, it's has an excellent chance to be successful. These basic three elements of a functional relationship apply to all human societies even allowing for cultural variations. Only 3 components are needed. They are:

1. An Environment
2. A Seesaw (creating Role A/Role B)
3. 2 Copartners, (creating Copartner A/Copartner B.

Let's compare each of these parts to a children's playground. What would it take to create a children's playground? You only need three distinct elements. They are:

1. An Environment, the physical location where equipment is located so the children have a place to play.
2. Various playground structures, such as slides, merry-go-rounds, rings, a sand box, etc.
3. Children to play on the various structures.

Unless all three parts are present and interacting in combination, you really don't have a functional children's playground. Please note the following:

- Without an environment, there is no place for the playground equipment to exist.
- Without playground equipment, there are no structures on which the children can play.
- Without children to play, lonely equipment sits idle in an empty location with no activity.

Everyone can understand how a children's playground is created based on these 3 elements. Now, use this example to see how human relationships closely follow this same setup. All relationships take place:

- In an Environment
- On a specific Seesaw Structure
- Between 2 Copartners.

The Environment is the same. Without some kind of environment, where is the relationship going to occur? In human relationships the interactions generally take place in external environments such as the home, a neighborhood, school,

Chapter 11: A Brief Outline of How Relationships Work

workplace, etc. Each of the Family, Social, and Work environments have classic areas where "normal" relationships take place.

To describe the structure aspect, we use the analogy of a seesaw or teeter totter. Most people are familiar with this playground equipment which is basically a board that balances at the center on a base. Each side of the empty seesaw represents a specific role that defines the relationship category.

Relationships are named based on the two roles being featured. These roles can have distinctly different purposes such as the Parent/Child or the Boss/Employee relationship. And, the same role can occur on both sides of the seesaw, for example in a Friend/Friend relationship or the Coworker/Coworker relationship.

For a human relationship to work properly, just like on a children's seesaw, there needs to be two people on either side to balance their interaction. In this case, we call the people at either end of the seesaw, the 2 Copartners. These are the real people who take on the role as determined by which side of the seesaw they sit. The term "Copartners" is used to represent the idea that the two people are working together so the relationship can function correctly.

A relationship of any type begins when two people get on a specific seesaw structure and play the role based on their side. As long as both people stay on this seesaw and interact, the instance of this relationship continues. If/when one of the Copartners abandons his/her role on his/her side, the relationship ends.

Using this model, we can describe any human relationship. As listed earlier, 12 classic relationships make up the everyday interactions of human society. The 3 main relationship types are Family, Social, and Work, each with their specific categories.

Each of the 12 structures, how they work, along with all the roles, rules, customs, etc. are precisely detailed in the book, *How Relationships Work*. Each relationship can be intentionally examined to understand specifically how the three components interact.

It's amazing how useful the HRW model is. Just plug in the basic information for the environment, seesaw, and people for the relationship you want to evaluate. As you describe each part of the model, it's easy to sense the dynamics for the specific relationship you are evaluating.

THE ENVIRONMENT CAN VARY

In general, each of the three types of relationships, Family, Social, and Work have typical locations in which they operate. However, the Environment can vary for any of the different relationships. For example, you could have three types of relationships occur in the exact same Environment, depending on the specific seesaw.

For Family, the usual environment is the home and the larger neighborhood where the home is located. The kitchen, living room, and bedrooms would feature heavily in Family relationships. The family environment is usually associated with the period when the children are growing up until they leave home. Grown children are still family of course, but the dynamics change. For *your* Family environment, think of the home in the neighborhood where you grew up.

Chapter 11: A Brief Outline of How Relationships Work

Each environment has unique factors which can influence the outcome of a relationship. For example, the home environment could vary from living in a safe neighborhood with lots of friendly neighbors to living in a car in a rundown area, surrounded by poverty without enough food to eat.

You may have grown up in the only home you've ever known. Or, your family could have moved 9 times before you were 12. Maybe you were brought up by parents working in a traveling circus or as missionaries in Guatemala. Each person's origin story of his/her home growing up is unique to them.

Social relationships take place in diverse environments such as schools, restaurants, religious centers, libraries, movie theaters, etc. Once you leave the house you are in your neighborhood. Where you go to school, church, synagogue, mosque is part of your social world. The places where you shop, visit, travel, or explore reflect your social environment.

As far as Work Relationships are concerned, the Environment can be any location where the exchange of services or money takes place. Typically, this is an office, warehouse, or store location. It could be as diverse as indoors, outdoors, at the top of a high-rise, under water, or out in the wilderness.

Wherever you normally perform your job duties represents your work environment. If you are an actor maybe your work takes place on a stage or a movie set where you pretend to be in Scotland even though you are actually in Prague.

THE ROLE REPRESENTS THE "IDEAL"

The Role being played on a relationship seesaw is a key aspect of any relationship because it defines the rules of how the role is played. For example, the teacher role would have a certain set of rules and the student role would have another set of rules. Each Role is a shorthand description that contains all of the Rules associated with that Role. Each Role has its unique set of Rules, which is why it qualifies to be placed in one relationship category over another.

Each relationship has a generic standard of behavior for the relationship roles and the rules for each role are similar among all human cultures. However, each human culture may include different nuances for specific roles and this too has a place in the model.

Being a Parent, whether in China or Morocco, is generically the same role. But there could be some customs that a parent from Morocco might follow, whereas one from China or Brazil, might have a different set of approved customs for the parent role.

COPARTNERS PLAY EACH ROLE

Each role in a relationship must be played by a real person. Until such time as real people are playing their correct role, a relationship has not been established. How well a person plays his/her role represents their skill as a copartner. Each Copartner brings his/her individuality to the Role. If a person playing his/her role does an excellent job, then s/he is fulfilling the rules associated with this role with a high degree of skill.

For example, the Parent role has an ideal set of rules. They are responsible to provide for the physical, emotional, and mental needs of a child. Know however, that there is a strong possibility that a specific Copartner, the actual person playing the Parent role, may not "perform" very well as the ideal parent.

Chapter 11: A Brief Outline of How Relationships Work

The Teacher role has an ideal role and set of rules to follow. Yet for all the training that teachers go through, it's unlikely that all your Copartners played their teacher role in an ideal way. Perhaps from your side, you may not have always succeeded in the ideal Student role either.

As regular people, we can only play a relationship role to the level of our mental/emotional maturity and training/experience in that Role. It's a goal we can strive for, but we don't often experience the ideal Copartner for most of our many relationships.

Let's talk about the Friend Role. If a person is good at playing the Friend Role, they are following a set of rules that everyone accepts as positive for a friend such as loyalty, honesty, and supportive interaction. If a person is a terrible Friend, then we can safely assume they are breaking all the important Rules of the Friend Role. For example, they are not loyal, not honest, and not supportive.

It's important to understand that each Role is neutral and represents the ideal. If you have been burned by people playing the "friend role", you might decide to hate the concept of a friend. You now avoid any aspect of your life that involves having "a friend" in the vain hope that you will never again be hurt.

If the person playing a role is not good, then don't blame the role. The role is a neutral standard based on ideal behavior. If an actor butchers the role of Hamlet on stage, we don't blame the role of Hamlet. We blame the actor who isn't playing the role properly. If your friend is not the "ideal" friend, then they are just a bad copartner. Another person could easily do an excellent job of playing the Friend Role.

Relationships are often an area where we "win some and lose some." Your individual experiences within various relationships may have differed widely from the ideal generic model. It's not that the ideal Copartner is impossible to find in the "real world." Many examples exist of relationships with ideal Copartners. These people, bless their hearts, seem to act according to the "normal" way a relationship role works best. It just seems like the positive ones you've witnessed are on seesaws with other people.

Assuming the Environment and Seesaw meet the minimum standards, the defining key to every relationship is the Copartner element. This is the actual person playing the Role on the other side of your seesaw together. We are going to take a slightly deeper look at the Copartner aspect of a relationship, but ultimately all the specific details are defined in *How Relationships Work*.

We can evaluate a Copartner based on three aspects. They are the:

    1. Copartner's Traits
    2. Copartner's Needs
    3. Copartners Tactics

Once you know how to evaluate these three areas of the person playing the Copartner Role, you will have a really good idea if they are a positive person or not.

COPARTNER TRAITS

Seven traits define how well a person does when performing as a Copartner. These traits are not simple random positives about a person that we put on our wish list such as "good sense of humor," or "extremely good looking," or "has a lot of money."

Specifically, these seven traits define how well a person plays his/her assigned role on the other side of your seesaw together. These traits define an objective standard by which to evaluate how relationship worthy a person might be.

Each Trait applies specifically to how a person acts (and reacts) in relationship situations. Know that you face these same evaluations yourself when playing your role in any relationship you enter.

If a Copartner is positive in all seven Traits, he/she will perform well on any relationship seesaw. Conversely, if the person manages to show all seven Traits as negative, this Copartner will sabotage any relationship Seesaw they are on.

These seven Traits are:

      a. Being Attracted
      b. Being Committed
      c. Being Genuine
      d. Being Trustworthy
      e. Being Emotionally Mature
      f. Having Communication Skills
      g. Having Problem-Solving Skills

Let's take a brief look at how each of these Traits determine the ability of a Copartner to play his/her relationship Role

BEING ATTRACTED

Being Attracted is how strong the feeling or sense of connection is with the other Copartner. It reflects how badly they want to be on the seesaw with the other person. Without this attraction, a Copartner will be unable to sustain the relationship because he/she will not:

SELF-Parenting For LIFE:

- Want to be on the seesaw in the first place
-     or
- Stay on the seesaw after they've experienced a bit of the relationship

A strong sense of attraction supports both Copartners in any category of relationship. This is required simply to get the relationship started. If even one, and especially both of the Copartners on the relationship seesaw lacks the Trait of Being Attracted, success for relationship is doomed.

Different relationships have different qualities for Being Attracted. For example, in Family Relationships, the attraction is based upon blood and family ties. In Social Relationships, the attraction is based on mutual admiration and sharing. In the Work Relationships, the attraction occurs due to financial needs or similar creative interests.

This can be painful, because you might truly be attracted to a particular person on a specific seesaw. But the attraction may only be from your side. It doesn't really matter which category of seesaw.

Let's say you really want to be the employee of a well-known business mogul. But for whatever reason he/she has no interest in being on the Boss/Employee relationship with you. Or you really would like to be the girlfriend or boyfriend of a particular guy or girl. But for whatever reason s/he has no interest in going out on a date. It could even happen in Family relationships. Once you are adults, if one or more of the siblings is not actually interested in getting together, there's not much you can do.

Chapter 11: A Brief Outline of How Relationships Work

BEING COMMITTED

Being Committed is the measure of a Copartner's willingness to invest time and energy on the relationship seesaw. It is also reflects the guarantee each Copartner gives the other that he/she will remain in the relationship. Being Committed implies the motivation each Copartner has to meet the needs of the other Copartner.

If only one Copartner is willing to meet the other's needs, the long-term value of the relationship will suffer. Being Committed means both copartners are willing and eager to give energy to the relationship. Yet each individual Copartner only has so much total energy to go around. Energy may be required for two relationship seesaws, but you only have enough energy for one. Thus, the Copartner's Trait of Being Committed can become a crucial test of your relationship priorities.

Ideally, each Copartner contributes an equal amount of time and energy (Commitment) to their relationship even if this energy assumes different forms. For example, one Copartner in a Work Relationship might put in 90% of the time and the other 90% of the money, but the contribution of energy is still considered balanced by both sides.

If only one Copartner puts in an unequal amount of time or energy, the relationship will be unbalanced, creating potential problems. What happens if only one person on a seesaw attempts to do all the work for both sides? That person will get really tired and besides, it won't work.

BEING GENUINE

Being Genuine is the willingness and honesty a Copartner has to communicate his/her true thoughts, feelings, and needs.

Genuine Copartners in relationships appreciate Being Genuine more than any other quality.

Copartners must be willing to be honest with each other. If one Copartner tries to camouflage his/her true thoughts, feelings, or needs, the relationship can only suffer. If a Copartner conceals his/her true thoughts, feelings, or needs from the other, the relationship will be superficial at best. If a Copartner expresses false opinions or values, the relationship only exists based on false pretenses.

Genuine Copartners do not hide their thoughts, feelings, or needs nor will they expend energy building facades. They are not evasive in conversation nor do they distort the facts about their job, accomplishments, income, age, marital status, or any other aspects of their life.

BEING TRUSTWORTHY

Being Trustworthy is the ability of a Copartner to be able to depend upon the other. This Trait is the foundation for building trust, which is an essential aspect of exchanging needs. If Copartners can't trust the other person riding on the relationship seesaw, how relaxed and comfortable will they feel? The betrayal of trust between Copartners is the ruin of any relationship.

Trustworthy Copartners will not reveal information given in confidence nor later use this information against the other. Nor do they criticize each other in public. Once trust has been established, Copartners are open and honest about any condition or fact in their lives. The Roles for every relationship seesaw benefits when both Copartners are trustworthy.

Chapter 11: A Brief Outline of How Relationships Work

BEING EMOTIONALLY MATURE

Being Emotionally Mature is the ability of a Copartner to balance his/her personal needs against the needs of the other person. If either Copartner is immature, their overriding concern for meeting their own needs can hurt the relationship over the long term.

Emotionally Mature Copartners are able to maintain a balanced perspective of needs within a relationship. They understand their own needs and motives and are aware of and sensitive to the needs and motives of their Copartner. They recognize the importance of the relationship structure and put energy into nurturing and protecting it. They also refuse to attempt relationships with Copartners having negative Traits.

Emotionally Mature Copartners have a positive sense of self-esteem, which includes self-caring and self-sufficiency. Since they recognize and understand their priorities, they use their energy and skills in a positive and fulfilling manner. Emotionally Mature Copartners are interested in enjoying and improving their relationships. Thus, they willingly expend energy to achieve this purpose.

Emotional Maturity is something that grows and expands with experience. If both Copartners are immature, being in a relationship is how they will learn and grow. Certainly, the high school Boyfriend/Girlfriend Copartner will be less mature than one in college, unless he/she didn't date in high school either. Each of us grow in wisdom and know-how by early experiences and practice in all our outer relationships. If you are working at your first job, your maturity will understandably be less than after one or two years at the position.

HAVING COMMUNICATION SKILLS

Having Communication Skills is the ability a Copartner has to share and express his/her personal thoughts, feelings, and needs. All people think, feel, and have needs, but this does not necessarily mean they can communicate them to others.

When a Copartner can accurately communicate what s/he is thinking, feeling, and needing to the other, then this communication has a chance to be received the way it was intended. The practice of positive Communication Skills by each Copartner helps to avoid problems and keeps any relationship free of stress. The deeper levels to the exchange of communication is detailed in the book, *How Communication Works*.

HAVING PROBLEM-SOLVING SKILLS

Having Problem-Solving Skills is the ability and willingness to resolve problems within a relationship. Relationships are a union Any conflict that is not resolved in a timely manner will cause the union to weaken. Since no relationship can be without conflict, Problem-Solving Skills are essential for a relationship to run smoothly. The style of Problem-Solving used by a Copartner has a strong impact on the quality and experience of the relationship.

Copartners with positive Problem-Solving Skills realize that most problems in a relationship are created by unmet needs. They understand the way to avoid problems is to communicate their needs honestly and openly on a regular basis with their Copartner. If a problem escalates into a major conflict, Problem-Solving Skills become essential for the bond's survival.

Chapter 11: A Brief Outline of How Relationships Work

SUMMARY ON TRAITS:

An attracted, committed, genuine, trustworthy, and emotionally mature Copartner who can communicate and has problem-solving skills will make positive contributions on every relationship structure s/he enters. Even if a relationship must end, a Copartner with positive Traits will minimize the harmful emotional and psychological effects that could otherwise occur.

NEEDS: THE MOTIVATION FOR A RELATIONSHIP

Needs, the second component of the human Copartner, provide the motivation each person must have to participate in a relationship. Each Copartner chooses a relationship structure based on his/her personal set of Needs. The desire to meet their Needs is why they enter a relationship in the first place. The fuel that makes the relationship run is the mutual needs as expressed by each Copartner.

Each relationship is designed to meet a specific set of Needs. Ideally, a Copartner chooses the relationship structure that best fulfills his/her personal Needs. If you took a group of strangers whose Needs were precisely known and grouped them together on a desert island, you could easily pick the exact category of relationship each would choose and with whom. Given the craziness of reality, things are not this easy in the "real world."

Relationships satisfy four categories of Needs. Learning to use these categories to identify your Needs will save you hours of wasted time trying to determine what is missing in your relationships. The four categories of Needs are:

1. Physical
2. Emotional

3. Mental
4. Relational

PHYSICAL NEEDS

Physical Needs are those that mostly involve the body and physiological processes. Eating, drinking, and sleeping are some examples of Physical Needs. With outer relationships the physical needs are either shared or exchanged by one Copartner with the other.

EMOTIONAL NEEDS

Emotional Needs are those that mostly involve feelings. The need to be loved, accepted, and nurtured are some examples of Emotional Needs. Each relationship is tailor made to provide the emotional needs corresponding to the Role played by the Copartner. If the other person you in a relationship with shows that he/she cares about you, this goes a long way to satisfying your emotional needs. And vice versa.

MENTAL NEEDS

Mental Needs are those that mostly involve thinking and logic. Outer relationships that encourage curiosity, the desire to learn, and the teaching of new ideas are some examples of Mental Needs that are provided by relationships. The Teacher/Student relationship is the classic example for providing mental needs. The Teacher enjoys teaching and the Student wants to learn. Work relationships can provide new learning activities and experiences that might not happen in any other way.

RELATIONAL NEEDS

Relational Needs are those that involve the 2 Copartner's interacting together with other people in groups. Sharing celebrations, holidays, and meeting with like-minded individuals are some examples of Social Needs. Specifically, Social needs are provided for a relationship when the Two Copartners relate and participate as part of a larger group.

One example might be when a girlfriend needs her boyfriend to accompany her to a wedding. Or when a child wants his parents to attend the school play or a baseball game. Perhaps the employees of a company need to put on a big promo party to impress potential customers. Basically, the interacting Copartners on whichever relationship seesaw are on become part of a larger group of social interaction than just the two of them.

Understanding a Copartner's needs in a relationship can be very difficult for some people. The easiest way to determine what your Copartner needs might be is to ask yourself the following questions, keeping in mind which relationship structure you are on:

1. What Physical Needs might (person's name) be trying to meet by playing the _____ role?
2. What Emotional needs could (person's name) be trying to meet by playing the _____ role?
3. What Mental need is (person's name) trying to meet by playing the _____ role?
4. What Relational needs can (person's name) meet by playing the _____ role?

SUMMARY ON NEEDS:

Needs are the spark that generate the energy to run a relationship. If you don't have the needs a relationship fulfills, you won't want to be on the relationship seesaw that fulfils those needs.

It behooves every SELF-Parenting practitioner to become familiar with the PEMR structure of physical, emotional, mental, and relational needs. Clarifying your needs within your SELF-Parenting relationship is the key to playing your role on your side of any outer relationship seesaw. This enables you to improve and strategize your outer relationship activities on your side of the seesaw.

The SELF-Parenting modules have many examples of clarifying needs between the Inner Parent and Inner Child. They add an extra dimension for both the Inner Parent and Inner Child to consider and agree on a plan of action with the best potential to fulfill mutual needs based on their role as one-half of an outer relationship.

There can be definitely be a conflict between the needs of the two inner selves when faced with the many options in outer relationships. In my experience it takes about two to five years for a SELF-Parenting practitioner to become comfortable with how each inner self understands the other in their Personal World. Only then does it become potentially achievable to pursue outer Relationship World needs and goals based on the combined cooperation of both selves.

Unless and until the two inner selves can rely on knowing what each other wants from outer relationships, the complexities of playing outer relationship roles gets lost in the dysfunction of the SELF-Parenting relationship.

Once the internal SELF-Parenting relationship is functioning correctly, the two selves can mutually cooperate to achieve outer relationship goals and needs.

Chapter 11: A Brief Outline of How Relationships Work

THE IMPORTANCE OF TACTICS: HOW YOU PLAY THE GAME

Tactics, the third and final component by which to evaluate a Copartner, are the methods and strategic choices used by each person to meet his/her relationship needs. The Tactics chosen by each Copartner are commonly evaluated as positive or negative.

Let's say a Boss wants an Employee to stay late. A positive Tactic would be to let the Employee know in advance and make the request optional. S/he would also give the employee the time needed to rearrange their personal schedule, make some needed calls, and plan around this request. A negative tactic for meeting the same need, would be to tell the Employee five minutes before the end of the day they are required to stay and threaten to fire the Employee if s/he doesn't comply.

The Tactics of a Copartner are closely linked to his/her Traits. When a Copartner uses positive Tactics to meet his/her needs within a relationship, that person likely has positive Traits. If a Copartner uses negative Tactics to meet his/her relationship needs, this person typically has negative Traits. This is a very accurate way to measure a person's positive or negative traits.

Another way of saying this is a person with negative Traits uses negative Tactics. Every Copartner has a mixture of positive and negative Traits. The ideal Copartners for your relationships will be the ones that use mostly positive Tactics when trying to meet their needs, as opposed to negative.

A typical example of negative Traits = Negative Tactics might be the story of Mary. Mary has the Trait of not Being Genuine. Her friend Lucy calls and asks her to go to a movie. Mary has a selfish need not to offend Lucy, but because she can't be genuine and just say that she doesn't want to go, she uses the tactic of telling Lucy she has a date. Her tactic is negative because she is lying. Since Mary has the trait of not being genuine, to her a little white lie is "no big deal."

The main reason Tactics are so important, besides the fact that bad tactics indicate bad traits, is that Tactics are often the first clue you get in a relationship that things are not going exactly as they seem.

Whenever someone starts a new relationship, they are typically extra careful to act in accordance with positive relationship values. Most people know what these positive values are and in the beginning, they can be quite skillful to present these values even if it's not their normal style. But after a while as the relationship continues it's harder for this person to maintain their façade if it's not part of his/her normal personality.

It generally takes about three months into an active relationship before a Copartner with bad traits begins to lose his/her ability to maintain the outer pretense of positive traits. This is when that person who was always so good at returning calls now starts to lose that quality. Or, little inconsistencies start to pop-up in explanations for being late or cancelling an appointment.

How many girls have a story about that "perfect guy" who later turned out to be married. Or the "ideal employee" who after a while just stopped coming into work without even calling in to announce they were quitting.

Traits are only something you learn about a Copartner after spending time on your seesaw together. If you know someone for just one day, or even a week/month, that person can make an excellent and convincing presentation of what they are like. This is one of the problems with long-distance relationships.

Chapter 11: A Brief Outline of How Relationships Work

You only see each other for some brief time in-between long absences. This makes it easier to hide negative traits.

Traits are revealed by how someone acts, not what they say or pretend on a superficial level. Each trait has positive or negative indicators that reveal a person's true feelings over time. For example, consider the trait of being attracted. If a person on your seesaw cannot seem to find time for you in his/her life, this is a sign that they are not that attracted. Maybe they say they are, and insist they want to get together with you, but they never follow through.

Each relationship has its own version of "being attracted" so there could be 12 different ways to judge. It's when you start to feel vaguely unhappy about a relationship and you begin to wonder what's going on, that you start putting two and two together based on tactics.

When you experience three or more "bad tactics" in short succession, this is a strong sign the person is beginning to reveal negative traits. It's actually a sad situation when you really like someone in any of the 12 relationships and now, they just seem to keep letting you down.

You will only realize this after more time and enough experiences that point to this conclusion about someone. It takes personal integrity, ideally gained from your SELF-Parenting practice, to admit a bad relationship to yourself and exit the seesaw at the soonest appropriate moment.

SUMMARIZING: YOUR COPARTNER (THE PERSON)

These chapters contain summarized details about the most important and complex element of a relationship, the Copartner, who is a combination of his/her Traits, Needs, and Tactics.

Defining these three areas as applied to a specific person gives you a shorthand method to evaluate any person with whom you are in a relationship. As explained, this is distinct from the Role that he/she may be playing.

The ability to make this determination is crucial to understanding (and evaluating) your personal relationships. For even more specifics and the deepest understanding of each of the 12 relationship structures, please consult your copy of *How Relationships Work*.

Chapter 12:
How SELF-Parenting Benefits Your "Outer" Relationships

Chapter 12: How SELF-Parenting Benefits Your "Outer" Relationships

Let's return to the focus of this book which is to understand how to best apply your daily practice of SELF-Parenting to living your life. As humans, our goal is to follow the ideal role for each outer relationship seesaw we are on. Hopefully each of our Copartners will also act according to the role they play.

As a SELF-Parenting practitioner, you coordinate your Inner Parent/Inner Child selves to play your "outer roles" on your half of the seesaw. For this you need a solid understanding of each role you play in your Relational World. You would be familiar with the rules for each relationship role and also do your best to follow them per your desires and abilities. Ideally your copartners will do the same, and life can be a happy experience for all concerned. Your mileage may vary.

To do this properly and skillfully as a SELF-Parenting Practitioner involves 3 aspects:

- You maintain your personal SELF-Parenting as consciously as possible on your side of the seesaw.
- You are as aware as possible of the needs of both inner selves.
- You use the same conscious communication skills learned within your internal SELF-Parenting practice to facilitate win/win problem-solving in your outer relationships

Here is the number one difficulty to watch for as a SELF-Parenting Practitioner which involves outer relationships and it's a big one. This knowledge will save you on the deepest level once you truly understand this.

Even if you perfectly follow the above three guidelines, your Copartner, the person on the other side of the seesaw may not. In which case, your outer relationship can fail through no fault or responsibility of your own. This is a very unfortunate aspect of relationships.

You can give 100% positive effort to an outer relationship. But you only control the 50% half that represents your side of the seesaw. If your Copartner on the other side, for whatever reason, does not fulfill his/her role in a positive way, your entire relationship can fail completely.

This can be VERY painful when it happens. If you can deeply know and understand if this occurs that it's not your fault, it helps a little. I also hope you would never be the person that does this to your Copartner for any relationship you are in.

Just like riding a seesaw on a playground, outer relationships work the same way. You can only control and manage your side. Let's say you sincerely and competently work your side of a seesaw with 100% integrity. If the other person decides to jump off your seesaw, you will still come crashing to the ground.

There can also be the situation where you believe you are on one type of seesaw, but your Copartner believes he/she is on a different seesaw. This causes an extreme relationship problem because the needs and reason for which you are on that seesaw are not going to be fulfilled. This can be hard to diagnose, even when you know about this potential problem. Only after the relationship fails, do you usually figure this out.

Another major problem occurs if a person from his/her side of the seesaw tries to control your side of the seesaw or wants you to do the work on their side. For a relationship to work correctly, each person is tasked to do their side and only their side on the seesaw. What happens if your seesaw riding partner

Chapter 12: How SELF-Parenting Benefits Your "Outer" Relationships

climbs off his/her side and comes over to your side just to help you out?

Another problem occurs when your Copartner refuses to put forth an equal amount of energy. These types of energy do not have to be the same. For example, in a work relationship both money and time are required for the relationship to succeed. One person could contribute more money and the other more time. Contributions do not have to be same in nature. They just need to be equivalent so both Copartners feel the relationship is balanced.

Another difficulty comes into play when seeking a successful outer relationship. Do you recall the four definable outcomes that can occur in your Inner Parent/Inner Child relationship? These same 4 potential outcomes occur with outer relationships as well:

- Lose/Lose
- Win/Lose
- Lose/Win
- Win/Win

Notice that three of them involve one side losing. Numerically speaking, three out of four relationship outcomes involve a loss. You might also say that three of them involve one side winning. A win for at least one Copartner in a relationship might seem positive but it's not really this way at all.

Here is the reality of an outer relationship dynamic. If either side loses, both Copartners lose. This may seem like an odd idea, but you need to know this about outer relationships. A truly positive relationship only occurs when both Copartners are winning; in other words, neither Copartner is losing.

An Idea For Your Consideration

Let's say you are in a relationship where you are winning, even if the other person is losing. You might be happy and this may feel good for a time. You might not even know your Copartner is losing if they don't speak up about it.

From the SELF-Parenting point-of-view, you could be so happy, that even when you eventually realize your copartner is losing, you find it easy to justify continuing the relationship. "If he/she wants to lose in our relationship, why should that bother me? I'm happy." However, problems will eventually come into play. Ultimately a relationship where either side is losing is not sustainable.

If you are winning in a relationship, why is this so bad? Any win is a win, right? Short-term winning may feel good, but it comes at a price karmically speaking. Here is an idea for your consideration based on the law of karma with which I'm sure you are familiar.

Let's say you have an account in a "relationship bank." Instead of money, it has point totals and it's your account only. Each person has their own account and they don't mix. The way this account works is as follows. For every relationship you enter, points are deposited into your account or taken out based on your sincerity and ability level from your side of the relationship seesaw.

The bank is keeping three scores. Each copartner has a personal account. In addition, their relationship also has an account which combines the two inputs from the copartners. The "relationship account" only exists as long as the two copartners are in a relationship. If the relationship ends, all the points

Chapter 12: How SELF-Parenting Benefits Your "Outer" Relationships

disappear. If the relationship continues, the points remain and float up or down per the relationship status.

For each copartner's individual account, the score is kept as follows. The percent of energy in which he/she participates with good intentions from her/his side, is the amount of plus points he/she earns for their account. Every time you positively perform a role on your side of a relationship, you accumulate positive points.

Each copartner's relationship contribution account is permanent and accumulative for every relationship they enter. The point score for a single relationship range from 0 to 100. But all the points a copartner has ever put in or taken out of a personal relationship are totaled. Point scores can be positive or negative.

Here's an example using the Neighbor/Neighbor Relationship. If you give 100% positive energy to your relationship as a neighbor, then you get to deposit 100 points in your "Neighbor Account." Your neighbor also has his/her own Neighbor account and their effort goes into his/her account. Let's say your neighbor gives 80% to their role as a neighbor.

Your relationship totals 180 points and dividing by 2 gives your relationship a score of 90%. This relationship is very positive. Here is another example involving a neighbor on the other side of the street.

Let's say you give 80% to your role but this Copartner only gives 20%. Now you can see that your total relationship score is only 100 and divide by 2 and you get 50% functionality. This is not enough energy to sustain the relationship. There are enough "points" to equal half a relationship which means the relationship is alive, but just barely. Even though the relationship itself is not that strong, you still get to add 80 points to your lifetime "neighbor relationship" bank account and this copartner can add 20.

All the energy YOU put into each role you play goes into YOUR relationship account at the bank. You have a Parent account, a Friend account, a Boss, a Coworker, a Sibling account, etc., an account for each role. When you do good, your role accumulates points, when you do bad, your account specific to that role loses points. As each person goes through life the bank keeps a running total for each account, parent role, friend, role coworker role, etc. and keeps a grand total.

The reason this scoring system works is that every person has an unlimited number of potential relationships. Yet they only have a finite amount of energy to keep all of them rocking back and forth. You could have 1000 relationship seesaws, but at some point, you will run out of time and energy to be a good copartner on every seesaw.

If you are winning, but the other person is losing, it might seem like you getting free points. But what is really happening is that you are "spending" points or using them up. If you have good karma, you are burning up your own points. If you have bad karma you are adding points to your future debt.

Eventually when he/she abandons their side, all of a sudden you won't be winning any more. When you are winning at the expense of someone else losing, this is a harder fall to experience when it ends. When the dust settles you will have used up points or built up a debt of points, and you still have no relationship.

Whenever a relationship ends with a loss, you lose all your external efforts for that relationship. However, the effort you put in does go into your personal "good karma" relationship bank

Chapter 12: How SELF-Parenting Benefits Your "Outer" Relationships

account. It either goes in your account as a plus so you have more positive accumulated savings, or it goes to payback what you owed from a prior relationship where you took advantage earlier.

When you are winning and the other person is losing (whichever relationship you want to name), you are using up prior accumulated points. Or even worse, you are increasing your debt for points you will need to pay back to balance your ledger on what you are currently borrowing/being loaned.

If you are always good from your side of the seesaw, you gain points in the long run even if you wind up losing in relationships with bad Copartners. However, this is not as satisfying as a true win/win relationship with a current seesaw copartner based on matching contributions.

The beauty of this accounting system is that it gives you a way to pay back your karma for relationships when you were less mature or knowledgeable than you are today.

The only true "winning" relationship in real time is a win/win relationship and this takes two cooperating copartners to make this happen. Interestingly, it is not even required that each copartner be consciously SELF-Parenting. It is completely possible for successful relationships for each of the 12 types between Copartners based solely on their outer interactions.

Perhaps in "the olden days" more people did what they were supposed to do according to tradition because it was the right thing to do. In today's society, everything is increasingly complicated, and each generation seems to complain regarding the new generation that the older values are gone. Essentially you have to evaluate each of your human relationship based on your own assessment.

SELF-Parenting For LIFE:

When you have the advantage of conscious SELF-Parenting, not only can you do a better job for each role you play, it enables you to protect you and your Inner Child from entering or remaining in any outer relationship where you can see the three elements aren't working in your favor. You certainly want to guard against losing in relationship as well as winning with your copartner losing.

This is a vital yet difficult skill to apply, because if you find yourself in a "toxic" relationship, one of your own two selves is getting some kind of need met. Because this part of you is willing to sacrifice your other self's dignity to remain in the "outer relationship" it remains in this toxic relationship. This impacts your SELF-Parenting relationship to the core. This could be either Inner Parent or Inner Child acting this way. You have to figure out which self is saying what in your own situation.

As a general rule, it will be your Inner Child who typically brings up outer relationship problems within your sessions. As the more natural self, it will be tuned in to whether your energy exchanges are fair and balanced. This is similar to the story of The Emperor's New Clothes, where finally it was a child, who cries out, "But he isn't wearing anything at all!" If your Inner Child complains about a relationship more than three times, then you can be sure there is a problem there you need to deal with as the Inner Parent.

The pace of modern life has become increasingly intense and there is no going back. Today's action-packed world presents many opportunities for conflict between one's personal goals and the needs required for successful relationship goals. Gaining in some areas of life may require sacrificing in others.

Each of us has to navigate these treacherous waters on our own. Many unusual factors can come into play such as adverse

Chapter 12: How SELF-Parenting Benefits Your "Outer" Relationships

weather events, social changes, the economy, regime change, etc. that are far outside the control of either copartner wanting to have a positive relationship. This is only one reason why the daily practice of SELF-Parenting is such a valuable addition to your overall psychological profile. It keeps you attuned to these various issues as you strive to move forward in your life.

Time, practice, and experience will be needed for you to grasp the importance and validity for using the HRW relationship evaluation system. The best way to start is by evaluating all your important relationships based on the three elements. As you practice, practice, practice, you will soon be far ahead of the rest of humanity in understanding How Relationships Work.

Your role as the Inner Parent in outer relationships is to be honest with your Inner Child and "keep it real" between your own two selves based initially on your half of any seesaw. That's all you can control anyway. At the same time, the Inner Parent generally plays the lead for both inner selves when it comes to interacting with your copartner in an outer relationship.

When you know something is not right, it's often up to the Inner Parent to make the tough decisions. It's also possible that the Inner Child could be willing to endure emotional hurt in the vain hope of keeping a toxic relationship afloat, but not always. Your Inner Parent can be just as guilty in this regard.

Basically, this comes down to an Inner Conflict on your side of the relationship seesaw, which as you know must be resolved using the 8 Steps of Inner Conflict Resolution as per the website at http://www.selfparenting/.com. Making tough decisions in regards to important outer relationships is an ongoing priority during your first 5-10 years. After this, you know what your Inner Parent and Inner Child like, and you protect yourself.

The next "World" we are going to evaluate represents the third crucial world to your existence as a SELF-Parenting practitioner. It is called your "Financial World." In this section, we are going to consider how financial considerations impact your SELF-Parenting relationship.

In this world it's up to you and your Inner Child to navigate the stormy seas of financial predators who are out to get all your money, leaving you with none, which is totally okay by their morals and rules. It's not a pretty world.

Chapter 13:
Self-Parenting in Your "Financial World"

Chapter 13: SELF-Parenting in Your "Financial World"

INTRODUCTION

Ideally, you are closing in on the concept that every decision you make in life is a SELF-Parenting decision. If so, congratulations. This cognition alone will serve you well your entire life. Combining the strengths and talents of your Inner Parent/Inner Child relationship serves you continually.

Through the practice of SELF-Parenting, you have an effective tool for differentiating between your Physical, Emotional and Mental selves. Next, you were introduced to the fundamental principles of how your Family, Social, and Work relationships operate.

Now we enter the third world crucial for your happiness, your Financial World. When you become skillful at knowing the personalities of your Inner Parent and Inner Child in regard to managing money, you will have the final link placing you firmly in the center of your core knowingness and experience as a human. Specifically, we are going to outline some principles around the complex and crazy world called "your money."

As a function of being alive, you necessarily engage in financial interactions. "Your money" means the money that enters and exits your Personal and Relational Worlds under your jurisdiction. This is "your money" in that if suddenly you were "not alive," all these particular transactions would disappear. As a SELF-Parenting practitioner, this is a vital area of concern for both inner selves.

WHERE YOUR "FINANCIAL WORLD" BEGINS

Neither your Personal nor Relational Worlds have money as a significant aspect of your interactions within them. When you want to differentiate between your three worlds, here is how to think of them.

- Your Personal World does not involve outer people (or money.)
- Your Relational World involves only one "outer" person but money is not a primary focus of the relationship.
- Your Financial World begins when money becomes the primary purpose of the process.

What do I mean when I say, "Money becomes the primary purpose of the process?"

Let's say you are hungry, (which is physical) and you want to buy some food. Money is not the purpose of eating. You just need some money to buy food as it's unlikely a store or restaurant will give you food just for asking.

Or perhaps you want to buy a book for your own mental needs or get your sister a gift for her birthday (a Family need). In each case money must be spent to fulfill these mental (Personal World) or family (Relational World) goals. Although money is required to complete these transactions, money is not the focus of these actions.

Your Financial World begins when money becomes the primary purpose or topic of concern. Typically, this involves spending, earning, or transferring money as a function necessary to survive and prosper in today's modern world. Managing money is beholden to all of us in major ways. We need to be open to confronting and handling this area of life. Your current style of SELF-Parenting is where all this begins for you.

Chapter 13: SELF-Parenting in Your "Financial World"

The topic of money may seem a strange one for a book that is outlining the optimum SELF-Parenting path to consciousness growth. It's not often these topics are mentioned in the same sentence. Be assured that your Personal and Relational Worlds are infused throughout with money transactions. To maximize your functional experience as a human, we identify and name money as your third area of individual responsibility.

In the same way that your Personal life is intertwined with your Relationships, money management is an important aspect of both these worlds. So much so, it becomes an important world in and of itself. Let's explore how your Financial World works from the perspective of SELF-Parenting.

Money is a well-known topic of concern in the "real world." The functional aspects of keeping accounts and managing money are standard textbook knowledge. You can get a college degree in managing money. It's also entirely possible "your money" could be expertly handled by you or someone else in your life without any conscious SELF-Parenting. Forgive me if you are already excellently organized regarding money as could occur through training or personal software like Quicken or Mint. If so, there is still much to explore related to finances from the SELF-Parenting point-of-view.

Know that your Financial World represents a universe where you can make serious mistakes that can hurt you personally for a long time. While it is quite unusual to make a mistake and wind up with more money, it is very common to act in your best interests as far as you know, and still lose vast sums of money (even future money) through ignorance or being cheated. This is not a good thing.

If you are just starting your journey for inner happiness through SELF-Parenting, I hope to provide a short-cut to understanding how important the topic of money is for your personal happiness. Ideally you will have an easier path to learning about this subject than I did. Hopefully, you can derive a strong basic knowledge about finances through my trials and tribulations as you go on to experience your own. Everyone is going to experience "learning situations" when it comes to money, just as in your other two worlds.

One major reason money is included in the "big three" worlds of SELF-Parenting is because if no one cares about YOU for any other reason, they will care about your money and you need to protect it. It's a "thing."

People and particularly Places have an unnatural concern about money. By people and places I'm including the higher up combinations of people such as businesses, corporations and governments. Before you were born, people started charging money for everything they could think of and get away with. Where you live, what you wear, what you do for recreation; the list goes on. Life wasn't always this way.

WHERE DID MONEY COME FROM?

Where did money come from? It's not a natural substance of this world, it's a man-made idea. In primitive societies, before the modern concept of money, human life revolved around survival, community, and human interaction. Early indigenous tribal cultures revered the natural world and did not place any part of it as having a "financial worth."

Everything was shared and the richest person in the village was the one who gave the most away providing for others. Nature and all its bounty was regarded as "wealth" and this was understood as given freely by God or creation. Nature was revered as the source of fresh air, soil, water, and food and was

Chapter 13: SELF-Parenting in Your "Financial World"

respected, even worshipped for all it provided. As the earliest humans, we innately understood our responsibility to venerate and nurture our natural earthly gifts and bounty.

There are conflicting theories to explain how the concept of money became such a major aspect of human life. The "classic" teachings on this topic may not be correct at all. The earliest beginnings of money supposedly revolve around the concept of barter. One person had something another one wanted, who had something that person wanted, so they traded.

The story goes that trading became bulky and eventually coins and paper money took over as a way of transporting money. But some potential holes exist in this theory. Early indigenous cultures did not necessarily originate this concept concerning money although they did devise ways of measuring wealth and exchanging resources.

Whatever it's true origin, the concept of money as a medium of exchange has now become the way we keep score in modern society. Now that everything has a unit cost, plans and decisions can be made about value and exchange. People can enter agreements based on the same numbers. Exchanges that are based on money are easier to keep track of and manage.

Modern principles around money began to change about 10,000 years ago as hunter gatherer societies were replaced by permanent landowners who wanted to protect what "they owned." They began claiming ownership over the natural resources and did not want random people coming in and taking over their "holdings."

Unfortunately, for many people in today's world, money has become the end all and be all of existence. Especially for governments of all kinds, it just seems to be the lowest common denominator by which they judge and care about people. It has also become easier to keep track of you and your money as a reality of modern life. Thus, this man-made concept of money has created a "third world" which each of us individual humans now have to deal with on a daily basis.

A related aspect of your Financial World is that it requires you to be aware of and protect "your money." If you don't, someone else wants it bad enough to take it from you for no reason whatsoever. They could do it in a flash and justify it completely. If you weren't already being protected by basic laws, they would already have all your money. They could even give you many excellent reasons why taking your money was exactly what they were supposed to do, in fact for your own good.

Also central to money is one day, at some point someone will expect you, perhaps your family or certainly the institutions of society, to participate in the spending, earning, and transferring of money. As a child within a family you may be shielded from such responsibilities. But as you mature you will eventually be expected to contribute financially to your own well-being as well as the financial well-being of others. That's just how life works in today's world. The more you understand money and how it flows, the better prepared you are, the more "successful" your SELF-Parenting life can be.

Again, the quality of your conscious SELF-Parenting Style is going to be the key to managing money. Be warned, just having a bunch of money is no solution or answer to money problems. Those who are born into money and never have to give it a second thought are often more crippled on the Personal and Relational levels than any of us can imagine.

Lottery winners are given massive sums in which to play with their money. You would think it would end their money problems forever. Not so. If not handled correctly, from a SELF-Parenting point-of-view, winning the lottery has proven to be no guarantee of future happiness once the elation from winning has worn off.

Even if your Personal and Relational areas of life are completely fulfilled, you can still have a host of troubles if your Financial World isn't right. Your ideal SELF-Parenting relationship with money is all three worlds in balance.

Theoretically money is your least important world, but it can be very helpful in supporting your needs and desires. If managed correctly, money is significant enough to guarantee your physical survival and provide reasonable opportunities to expand your Personal and Relational Worlds.

Many aspects of your money management will be colored by your Personal and especially your Relational environment. How you think/feel about money, how your family acts about money, what your culture encourages about money are all factors that drill deeply into your SELF-Parenting style long before you are handed the keys to your Financial World. And you certainly can't depend on your parents or even "financial experts" to be your best teachers about money.

Chapter 14:
Managing Money in Your Financial World

Chapter 14: Managing Money in Your Financial World

WHY DO WE NEED MONEY IN THE FIRST PLACE?

The best way to describe money is as a medium of exchange. Whatever material is used as money is given a value by the people that exchange it. Clam shells were a medium of exchange for remote Indonesian tribes as recently as last century as well as by some tribes of American Indians. Gold and silver seems to have held a universal appeal as having worth although it's hard to imagine why.

Essentially "money" is anything that your culture says has a value and is transferable to others. In today's modern world each country has a unit of currency. The US dollar is a unit of monetary value which can be exchanged with the other units from other countries. So basically, money is a medium of exchange and can be measured by and in numerical units of value. As it turns out, you need money to buy things.

If money is just sitting in a pile somewhere it doesn't have any value at all. It's just sitting there. You can't eat it or use it to put a roof over your head. The true value of money begins when you have some and start flowing it around to get something you want from other people/places such as food or a place to sleep. This is where it became important to give money a unit of exchange, so you can keep track of it properly flowing in or out of your life.

The following chapters discuss "your pile" of money and how best to manage it from the SELF-Parenting point-of-view. Think of the "real world" as being surrounded by an ocean of money. Although you can't have all of it, you can strive for as much as you can handle to become part of your "personal money." As part of being human you are invited to swim as deep as you like in this gigantic ocean of money.

SELF-Parenting For LIFE:

WHERE DOES YOUR MONEY BEGIN?

Based on a very simple analogy, your personal Financial World is created by two bathtubs. As part of your entry into this world you were assigned two bathtubs for the duration of your life for an important purpose. They are used to store your personal collection of all your financial activities as will soon be described. One bathtub holds all the money you currently own. The other contains all the money you currently owe. Your personal portion that you control of the vast money ocean are stored between these two bathtubs.

You have personal jurisdiction over your two bathtubs of money. Every person on the planet also has their version of these two bathtubs for which they are responsible. The contents of all bathtubs added together equals the ocean of money. All the money in the world can be said to exist in some person's or place's pair of bathtubs.

To keep track of these flows, you need a scoring system. Such a system appeared on the scene about 500 years ago at least as far as Western culture is concerned. The system used to keep a record of money flow in today's modern world is called double entry bookkeeping. It involves a somewhat complicated system for setting up various financial accounts.

An "account" is simply a name for a location where your money is counted and stored. Your skill at managing the flow of money in and out of your accounts is called money management. Once all your accounts are properly set up, if you follow the rules of double entry bookkeeping, any person or place who knows accounting rules can understand and follow the flow of money in and out of your life. This seems simple enough so far.

Chapter 14: Managing Money in Your Financial World

The rules of double entry bookkeeping are known and followed by businesses, banking, and government offices, etc. They ideally follow strict protocols, so their accounting procedures can be examined and verified by outside parties based on what are loosely called accounting standards. To track money correctly, it is tabulated and stored in locations called accounts as mentioned in the prior paragraph.

There are many ways money can flow in and out of your life. You can earn it, spend it, borrow it, save it, or loan it to name some major categories. To illustrate a point about accounts, let's use an example from one of these flows to show the value of accounts. We will start with the flow of earning money.

Let's say you earn money in at least three ways: chopping wood, cutting hair, and driving a taxi. It wouldn't be good to put all the money you earned from each method into one big account. If combined in one account, it would be too hard to know which money came from which source of earning. What happens if one day you start selling popsicles? Since it's earning, this money still needs to be added to your Earning account.

Since there can be so many ways to earn money, the custom has become to give each method of earning money its own account so earning can be kept track of properly. It this situation you will have an Earning Account for chopping wood, cutting hair, and driving a taxi. You can even add one for selling popsicles. All the various ways you can earn money are given their own named account for record keeping. Then, all the individual earning accounts flow into one big Master Earning Account.

Maybe you stopped earning money chopping wood last year and you don't expect to earn money chopping wood ever again. In this case you can close that account (saving it somewhere) without messing up your Master Earning Account. Every time you come up with a new way to earn money, it gets its own named account for the duration of its useful life.

As this system evolved it became easier to call each of various ways you earn money, sub-accounts. Then you can keep calling your main earning account the Master Earning Account. This works the same way for all your flows of money such as spending, earning, borrowing, loaning, or saving money, etc.

The movement of money in or out of your life is tracked from the sub-account where it originates and is then placed in the sub-account where it goes. Then the sub-accounts are totaled in the Master Account for that category. Describing and tracking the flows of money between all these different accounts is called accounting. Who knew?

In the double entry bookkeeping system, money can't just appear out of nowhere. You can't have one account where money just suddenly appears. As soon as money appears, the double entry bookkeeping automatically forces the creation of two accounts used to explain:

1. Where it came from, and
2. Where it went to.

These accounts balance each other with an equal but opposite action taking place in one of the other accounts. The numbers in these two accounts must equal each other or else there is an error in the accounting. I'm guessing this is why they call it Double Entry Bookkeeping.

To make this even simpler, all this money action starts with a "FROM account," from where the money starts its flow and ends up in a "TO Account" which is where your money ends its flow. As a person responsible for managing your own personal money, this is bottom line, the easiest way to understand the flow of money in to and out of your life.

Managing your money is a concern for both your Inner Parent and Inner Child. Theoretically your Inner Parent is the rational self, although it can be clueless about money as well. For the purposes of this discussion I'm doing my best to describe the flow of money in terms your Inner Child can understand. Like many life concerns, once your Inner Child gets a solid understanding of a complex topic, it can motivate decisions that the Inner Parent will find easy to fall in line with.

HOW MONEY FLOWS: INTRODUCING THE BATHTUB/SINK THEORY

As a SELF-Parenting practitioner, you already know money can potentially be a complex topic. It's a numerically based system, involves math, and is abstracted from daily living. Some people hate "all this money stuff" so much so that they refuse to even look into the topic at all.

Other people love money so much they squander the rest of their SELF-Parenting existence with their constant concerns and scrabble for money. We are going to take the middle path that money is a "world" where we need to live. We want the inner voices of our SELF-Parenting Style to understand and manage our flows of personal money to our best advantage. Ultimately if you manage money carefully, you can put all your money concerns on automatic and never think about it again.

This next section introduces an explanation of money designed to be very basic. The verbal descriptions (written words) are designed for your Inner Parent to understand, guide, and supervise your financial planning.

SELF-Parenting For LIFE:

The actual terms themselves, The Bathtubs/Sinks Theory, invite your Inner Child to create its own internal perspective using creative imagery.

Thus, both inner selves can apply the strategies of this system to manage the flow of your "personal money" together. Technically, this is not exactly the way that Double Entry Bookkeeping works. But if you and your Inner Child can standardize your personal financial management on the Bathtubs/Sinks System, you'll be excellently placed to understand Double Entry Bookkeeping when the time comes.

How Does My Money Flow?

For money to begin flowing anywhere, it must be resting somewhere from which it can start flowing. As a free gift for reading this book up to this point, you have been given two large bathtubs. These are conceptual bathtubs; they exist in the outer world even though they don't exactly take the shape of a physical bathtub.

Contained in these two bathtubs are all the past results of all your prior financial activities. How full or empty each bathtub is provides an up to the minute "score" that rates your success at managing money. These two bathtubs are called your Master Accounts. A Master Account is simply a big holding tank that contains all your financial transactions of a similar nature.

All your past money management is complete. All your prior money flows have come to rest. Your bathtub totals now sit in their resting state based their shorthand name. These bathtubs contain the exact financial value of all your prior financial activities up to now to the penny.

Chapter 14: Managing Money in Your Financial World

The two bathtubs currently holding your money have names. They are called your Assets and Liabilities Bathtubs. To understand how your "personal money" flows, you need to understand these two bathtubs since they are the foundation of your money world.

Your personal Assets and Liabilities bathtubs are also the source wells for all your future financial transactions. Even if you never knew this before, every prior financial transaction is easily calculated, and the results are currently stored in one or both bathtubs.

WHAT ARE ASSETS? THE ASSET BATHTUB

The first bathtub you now have holds all your personal Assets. An Asset describes something you own which has a financial value to other people as well. Something called cash money is clearly the number one asset. But assets can also be things like your car, furniture, paintings, stocks. Basically, anything with financial worth that could reasonably be expected to be purchased by others with an agreed value is an asset. Any Asset you control is stored in your Asset Bathtub.

Assets have a few designations; one is liquid and the other is fixed. When an asset is "liquid" it means your asset can be quickly and easily converted to cash. Examples of this are checking accounts and stocks. "Cash is king" as the saying goes. It is the most liquid asset possible.

When an asset is "Fixed" it means that although it has a clear monetary value it cannot be easily converted to cash, if at all. Examples of Fixed assets are real estate, furniture, lawn equipment, and grandma's silverware collection.

Fixed assets can have a high personal value. They are yours to do with what you will. You may have a beloved guitar that is an asset to you. You may have many other items that are assets to you, but they may not have a measurable and easily convertible financial worth. These could be referred to as "personal" assets.

For example, you may have the ticket stubs from your first date ever with your fantastic spouse of 30 years. These mementos mean the world to you and if you lost them it would be traumatic for a while. They are an asset to you because of their high emotional value.

But they may not be of financial worth to anyone else unless you happen to be part of a famous movie star couple, hopefully involved in a vicious divorce. Or, perhaps they are tickets 1 and 2, to the first ever Beatles concert held in the US.

If not of unusual interest, personal or private assets are typically not included in the day-to-day conversation as part of your "personal money" unless they can easily and clearly (keyword easily) become cash through a legitimate sale of some kind.

Another way of categorizing assets is "short term" and "long term." Short term assets are said to be spent or transitioned in less than a year. Long term means assets you control that may take time to show their value. It may even be that you aren't interested in selling because you want to keep them for a long time. These terms are typically applied for more complex business evaluations.

As far as your "personal money" is concerned, liquid assets are anything you own that can be easily converted to cash. As mentioned, everything you have like this right now, can be said to be sitting in your Assets Bathtub.

WHAT ARE LIABILITIES? THE LIABILITIES BATHTUB

This other bathtub holds all your personal Liabilities. In the simplest form your Liabilities are any money that you owe. Typical examples are credit card debt, installment loans, and money that was loaned to you by a friend you no longer have.

If you owe money to anybody for any reason, this is currently sitting in your liability bathtub. You could owe a person, place or a penny account. By "penny" we are referring to a monetary account of some kind. You may simply owe money to an account somewhere. The person or place may not be a significant part of the transaction. One example of this idea is a student loan. If you have an outstanding student loan, this is a "penny account" to which you owe money.

You Assets and Liability Bathtubs are repository accounts. This means they are like storage accounts. They reflect the total sum of contents for each of your bathtubs as lying around passively at its current level. Think of this as if they were filled with water like a real a bathtub.

The contents themselves don't do anything. They just sit there waiting to be used by moving their contents around. If you were gone tomorrow, the current contents of your two bathtubs would stay exactly the same until someone came along to take them over.

The reason these two bathtub accounts are the most important, is because they are the only accounts that matter if someone wants to know the total worth of your Financial World on a numbers basis.

By subtracting the total numerical value of all your liabilities from the total numeric value of all your assets, you arrive at your "net worth." This number reflects how much money you have on that certain date. Whatever the number is in your "net worth" is the score of your "Financial World" as far as the "real world" is concerned.

Chapter 15:
What If Money Was a Board Game?

Chapter 15: What If Money Was a Board Game?

If money was a board game, it might come in a box with the following parts.

- A board representing the playing field and 4 Pieces.
- Two bathtubs for Storing Money
    - One is your Asset Bathtub
    - One is your Liability Bathtub
- Two Sinks for Working with Money
    - One Sink is for Earning Money
    - One Sink is for Spending Money

In this game, your life is the playing field. And you have just learned that two of your pieces are the two bathtubs filled to their current level as of today.

Next, we are going to discuss the additional pieces which we are going to call two Sinks. Your "sink activities" are where the daily, weekly, monthly and yearly action of this game takes place as far as spending and earning money.

WHERE DOES SELF-PARENTING COME IN?

So far, we have just described the playing field and the 2 bathtub pieces. The first the rule of this game is that it is the responsibility of your Inner Parent to track and manage the flows of money in and out of your two bathtubs. The second rule is to track this money to the penny. This rule is so that you held to an agreement of integrity between you and your Inner Child.

This is a high bar to reach and you can't even pretend to achieve. If this idea of "tracking your money" to the penny, is new to you don't stress about it right now. Lots of people track their money to the penny, or whatever theirs country's unit of money. And they don't even consciously practice SELF-Parenting. It's something at least some people have done throughout the centuries. In the modern culture it can be done with just a small amount of attention and care.

Ideally you do this with full cooperation between your Inner Parent and Inner Child. The first reason is that you want to know this information yourself and you want it to be accurate. A second reason is that you may be compelled by the outer rules and circumstances of your culture or country to validate how much money you earn or spend for governmental purposes. If you need a third reason, it's so you don't have to ask anyone else to do it for you.

Tracking the flow of money in and out of your life is something that becomes important after two stages of SELF-Parenting practice have occurred:

1. Your Personal World is in order
2. Your Relational World is in order.

Let's assume that over the first 2-5 years of SELF-Parenting you get a really good understanding of your Inner Parent and Inner Child. During the next 5-10 years you begin to apply what you've learned to your outer relationships and eventually you start feeling comfortable about your "relational world." Now, after 5-10 year of quality relationship interaction with your Inner Child, you will certainly experience the need to manage your money as regards your future moving forward. If you can start earlier, so much the better.

Each SELF-Parenting practitioner will have his/her unique life experience leading to conscious money management, so this progression is a vast generalization. Maybe you grew up poor so before you even began SELF-Parenting you were determined to earn lots of money. Maybe you never really thought about money too much, but now you find yourself in a major debt

Chapter 15: What If Money Was a Board Game?

situation from which you have to extricate yourself. Maybe you unfortunate enough to be a trust fund baby, Whatever your situation, eventually you come to a point where managing your money is an obvious concern and the next step in your life mastery.

As mentioned, the money game has four "pieces" to deal with. The first two, Assets and Liabilities, have been briefly covered; they represent the repository accounts.

The final two parts of the game is the playing part. These are play the money game based on your actions that involve the spending and earning of money. These we call "Sink Activities" as when getting your hands in the sink. These reflect the daily, weekly, monthly, and yearly activities taken by you when the primary purpose is money.

By this is meant, if you don't pay the money, you don't get the goods or services. If you do pay the money, you do get the goods or services. You can use money to buy any amount of time, goods, and services you can afford. However, if you have no money, you cannot buy the time, goods, or services that you want.

The activities in your Money World can be summed up with two words. You are either Spending money or you are Earning money. Spending money is the act of purchasing some time, product, or service from a person or place. Strictly because you have the money, you do or have almost any experience you can think of. As long as you pay.

Earning is when you give of your time, goods, or services performing some activities, for one reason and one reason only, to earn money. It's the exact opposite of Spending. The key to both these transactions is that without money, the events do not happen. It is the money alone that fuels, not only the purpose of the relationship, but it guarantees that the time, products, or services will be delivered, take place, come into being. Without money, the transaction does not occur.

This puts money in a peculiar situation. If you become devoted to earning/making money you realize that money can buy you lots of the experiences you are looking for, which would not take place naturally on their own without money. Along with that gift comes the financial reality that if you don't pay close enough attention to your money flows, you might find yourself at the wrong end of a bad situation.

In the Bathtub/Sink Theory your transactional money activities take place in the Sinks where you mix and stir your financially related elements. Then you have your action sinks called the Spending and Earning Accounts.

All the actions in your "Sink Accounts" flow to an asset or liability bathtub. There will be more about Spending and Earning in upcoming chapters, but first you are about to learn the number one SELF-Parenting Practitioner Money Tip of all time!

THE SELF-PARENTING PRACTITIONER'S NUMBER ONE MONEY TIP (OF ALL TIME!)

The number one SELF-Parenting Money Tip I can share is to read the book, **Your Money or Your Life**, by Joe Dominguez. Study this book as if your financial life depends upon it, which it does.

In a similar way that **Handbook to Higher Consciousness** is recommended in the mental section, this godsend of a book explains all the major issues you need to know and understand to manage and monitor your money. Simply read and follow

Chapter 15: What If Money Was a Board Game?

everything in this book. This is huge. This tip will update your life big time. Are you ready?

The methods and procedures in ***Your Money or Your Life*** provide the main ideas and tools by which you can build your financial world in a predictable way that will never fail once you internalize the process. It has "big picture" insights as well as "nitty gritty" details. If you haven't heard of this book, you'll thank me later. If there was a way to summarize this book so you wouldn't have to read it, I would have tried. It's not truly possible to summarize this book. You just need to read it and do what it says to get the results that it promises.

Learning to manage your money properly is easier than it might sound but depending on your current financial circumstances it could be challenging but you can do it. Please listen and take this the right way. This is a clear case where it's your Inner Parent's job on its side of the seesaw to act and follow through. If you don't do this, it's your Inner Parent's "fault."

This is definitely not being stated from a perspective of blame. It's just a reality within the dynamics of your SELF-Parenting. Your Inner Parent is responsible for managing your money. It's possible that your Inner Child could energize and motivate you to care intensely about money management, but it's your role as the Inner Parent to follow through with the action steps.

Even if your Inner Child demands that your money be managed perfectly, it's not going to happen unless your Inner Parent does what it needs to do. The Inner Parent is meant to be the responsible self. If it doesn't do the actions, it's not going to get done. Also, the Inner Parent can do this task very competently without much help from the Inner Child.

Yet know that the energy and qualities of both selves are ultimately needed to manage money in a conscious manner. This is very much like both inner selves cooperating for success in your Personal and Relational Worlds. With money however, your Inner Parent has eighty percent of the responsibility to manage your money correctly and your Inner Child has twenty percent of responsibility to contribute from its side. Ultimately, from the SELF-Parenting point of view, the heavy lifting for money management lies with the Inner Parent.

Here's one example of such a responsibility. A key recommendation from *Your Money or Your Life* is tracking every penny that comes in or goes out of your life. It's your Inner Parent's side of the seesaw to be responsible for this. No blame, just the reality of the situation.

It's your Inner Parent's job to "track your money." It's not even a hard job. It just has to be done and when done right this becomes a lifelong habit. It's simply not the Inner Child's responsibility on his/her side of the seesaw. It would be like asking a five-year-old to pay the family's household bills.

Your Inner Parent is responsible to take charge and introduce this new habit into your current lifestyle. When you do, you'll have it down and it will be no big deal. If not, the accountability (get it?) lies solely with your Inner Parent.

This is exactly the same as keeping a food diary once you become serious about managing your weight. To change the way you eat, you must know when, what, and how much you are actually eating. Keeping a food diary is the necessary action needed to be taken by the Inner Parent to increase your self-awareness. This list is how you connect the thought currents flowing between the 2 selves wanting do something about your

Chapter 15: What If Money Was a Board Game?

eating patterns. If you have no list of food eaten (contributed by the Inner Parent), you have nothing to work with.

With money, you need to know what your numbers are as far as earning and spending. Don't let this put you off. Tracking your money is such an easy thing to do once you get started and the benefits pay for themselves in real dollars almost immediately. That's right. You can start making more money simply by tracking your money.

Numbers are how you keep score. They are meaningless in and of themselves. Any number, whatever it is, only has meaning to you and your Inner Child. Knowing the exact numbers is the necessary step that gives your Inner Selves the energy to do something about your spending patterns. It's basically your starting number. You need to know where you are starting from to get where you are going to. It is a neutral event as far as the world is concerned. Only you add meaning to it.

Tracking your exact outflows and inflows of money enables you to categorize and summarize your transactions into their various categories such as food, shelter and travel. *Your Money or Your Life* will show your Inner Parent and Inner Child how to review your spending and earning categories each month.

With the added insight of your conscious SELF-Parenting style, you'll evaluate each of your earning and expense categories. Both Inner Parent and Inner Child will consider each transaction and mutually agree on the value you received based on the amount of time it took you to earn the money for that item or activity.

Did you just catch that big hint about how money management works? Most of us spend our TIME performing an activity to make money. Our personal TIME is the price we pay (along with wear and tear on our body, emotions, and mind) in exchange for having money to spend on our needs.

By reading *Your Money or Your Life*, you will learn, through careful record keeping and evaluation, how much money you earn per hour. It's not just what your paycheck says. It also involves all the TIME and expenses you lose forever because you happen to work at that specific job.

Let's say 10 dollars is how much you earn per hour. This means, if you buy something that cost $20, this item cost you exactly 2 hours of time from your life. If your rent is $1000 a month, then your cost in TIME is 100 hours of your life each month. The average count of hours in a month is 730. If you subtract 100, that's now 630 hours you have left to do anything else you might like. Once you convert all your money outflows to hours worked, you finally learn why and how you don't have time to do anything in your life except work.

The free TIME that you spend at your own leisure, with zero concern about the financial cost, are your most precious life hours. As you learn to evaluate each of your expenses in terms of hours of time exchanged for your life energy, your two selves will become more interested in spending your mutual TIME as efficiently as possible.

One of the ways to do this is by not spending money on frivolous items which, when you really consider it, don't bring you much inner happiness. When both your Inner Child and Inner Parent finally comprehend that the money you are spending, which took so long to earn, is not returning an equal value, these decisions will be much easier to make.

Your Money or Your Life does an excellent job of helping in this one area alone. Just get a copy right away and follow each

Chapter 15: What If Money Was a Board Game?

step as the book suggests. If you don't have the money, it's at your local library.

In this way, it's like following the Ten Steps to Intermediate SELF-Parenting, except it involves your money. The book makes it super easy to follow each step and soon you will be able to clarify and align your money flows as well as any financial professional. Your money hassles will reduce over time and eventually disappear.

GAZINGUS PINS

Another interesting tidbit to tease you with from *Your Money or Your Life*, is the category of spending the author describes as your "Gazingus Pins." This is basically a made-up word for any category of item for which you are spending real money even though you already have a large collection of "Gazingus Pins" in your drawer (or wherever) at home. This could be any kind of item whatsoever.

Currently, you have an overabundance of Gazingus Pins. Yet you are susceptible to buying more and don't even know it. In the book, he talks about one lady with a bureau full of identical sweaters that she never wore. Shoes are another good example. Many people have shoes they've only worn once, and yet they still go out and buy more shoes. Magazine subscriptions or books you buy but never read are another common category.

A Gazingus Pin is something you buy over and over, even though you already have a lifetime supply. You are doing this unconsciously and it's an energy leak in your life where not only your money but more importantly your personal TIME is being drained away. As you closely examine your spending patterns, eventually you will discover YOUR unconscious patterns for buying Gazingus Pins.

SELF-Parenting For LIFE:

Once you become aware of your Gazingus pins purchase patterns you'll stop, but not until you recognize it via your own SELF-Parenting awareness. Even if someone points this pattern out to you, you still probably won't stop or act on it. This is just one more reason why writing down your daily expenditures and reviewing them once per month is so important.

It doesn't feel so good once you finally realize how much of your Inner Child's personal time is being squandered to pay for Gazingus Pins. It feels really good once you start applying this amount towards your preferred financial (personal and relationship) goals.

Your Money or Your Life provides all the tips, tricks, nuts, and bolts for managing your money. Reading and applying its principles and ideas will be the most financially rewarding time you have spent up to this point in your SELF-Parenting career. A plethora of books promise financial insights and there are some good ones out there. This book has all that you need to achieve financial independence.

Let's return to the Bathtub/Sink Game so your IC and IP can understand your money flows on a deep enough level to make some truly positive changes.

Chapter 16:
The Sinks: Money Action Accounts

Your Sink Accounts

The Sink Accounts are where you perform your daily actions spending and earning money. Your bathtubs are sitting underground somewhere. They are out of the way, hidden from your daily view.

Whenever you spend or earn money, you do so "in the sink" where money gets moved around by your Inner Selves from one bathtub to another. Imagine it's like you are actually handling the money and passing it around as if washing it in the sink.

Again, we are discussing these activities on a primal human SELF-Parenting level, so both selves can truly internalize these activities you perform daily. Your Spending Sink is where you got to spend the money that both selves work hard to earn. Since spending is a natural sink activity, you learn to observe and manage the ways you spend your money.

Why Are We Spending Money?

Here is a helpful idea you may find useful to understand all the various areas where you spend money as part of living. The categories where you likely spend money are:

1) The Physical areas of your life
2) The Emotional areas of your life
3) The Mental areas of your life

There's also another category where money can be spent that involves the:

4) The Family areas of your life
5) The Social areas of your life
6) The Work areas of your life

Chapter 16: The Sinks: Money Action Accounts

Are you starting to get the big picture?

The whole point of money is to enable you to navigate and manage your real life (i.e. your Personal and Relational Worlds). Your money is not your life, but it enables you to live your life.

Managing your money properly supports your goals and values for living, not the other way around. Once you have money under your control and are using it consciously to live your ideal life, you will find your day-to-day concerns with money slip into the background.

If you approach money correctly, it does lend itself to being put on a systematic autopilot. I'm not saying it's easy, but it can be done. The outside world sort of conspires against you in this regard. Your best chance to achieve this state is when you learn to use your SELF-Parenting Style to guide and manage your relationship with money which is taking place right now.

Let's take a closer look at these categories of spending based on terms with which you are already familiar.

PHYSICAL AREAS OF YOUR LIFE

Here we are talking about the basics: food, shelter and clothing come to mind. Transport costs are a physical consideration whether you take the bus, drive a car, or ride a bicycle to where you want to go. In today's world, all forms of transit other than walking or running require money. This was an easy one for society to monetize.

Many of your monthly expenses fulfill physical requirements such as food and rent. There's no way out of spending money in these categories. You spend money on Physical Expenses such as:

- Food
- Travel
- Car Expenses
- Shelter
- Health care
- Laundry / Clothing
- Utilities
- Etc.

EMOTIONAL AREAS OF YOUR LIFE

The emotional areas predominantly represent your Inner Child's areas of desire. Here, we are talking about activities and things that make you happy on an emotional level such as listening to music, watching TV/movies, and reading books/magazines.

You may enjoy nature, but you have to get there somehow, or pay to enter, or purchase camping gear, or pay fees for overnight stays, etc. Just the act of spending money creates an endorphin "feel-good" quality all by itself.

There is a good chance that you spend way more money for emotional pleasures than you realize which leaves less for your Physical or Mental budgets. As part of your monthly evaluations you can often figure out less expensive approaches to enjoying your emotional pursuits.

One example if you really think about it is, you can essentially listen to music for free on the radio or internet. This means saving a lot on individual CDs, not to mention all the clutter and storage costs that hard copies create. Or if CDs are a must for you, there are certainly lower cost ways to obtain massive used CDs at rock bottom prices.

It's also possible you are NOT spending money for the purpose of emotional satisfaction which could vastly increase your emotional fulfillment. If so, this is an area for future exploration.

Connecting to your emotional spending is a key function of your Inner Child and Inner Parent relationship. Money you spend on Emotional Expenses are: (This is just a minimal list of possibilities. Add your own.)

- Music
- Entertainment
- Movies
- Grooming
- Gifts
- Travel
- Eating out
- Etc.

MENTAL AREAS OF YOUR LIFE

The mental areas for spending money are more about your Inner Parent guided pursuits such as studying, learning, or trying to figure out worldly systems for living life. There are costs associated with going to school, purchasing books, studying with a guru, etc. You get the idea.

It can be very helpful as you assign your personal expenses into these categories of spending. It makes the specific details of your expenses more clear and gives you another perspective to evaluate their relative worth when compared to other spending options. You may think of yourself as a highly mental and evolved person. Yet you find all your money going towards pizza and beer as opposed to your desired mental pursuits.

Some of your Mental Expenses may revolve around:

- Software
- Seminars/Training Classes
- Books
- Licenses
- Printing
- Advertising
- SELF-Parenting Modules
- Etc.

RELATIONAL SPENDING: FAMILY AREAS

Growing up as a child you are unlikely to understand the flows of money swirling around you. However, you will surely and accurately sense any general vibe of family money interactions and incorporate them subtly into your unconscious SELF-Parenting Style. Before you come of age, start dating, or become a parent, your Financial World will have already begun to coil around your Personal World tightly like a python.

Becoming a parent creates and accelerates new responsibilities for spending and earning money in your Family World. Now financial considerations truly become real, due to the ongoing family responsibility of providing for your children. And children create a multitude of ways for you to spend money like no other. Maybe you didn't realize the extent of this when you were a child, but you certainly will if you become a parent.

Some young parents understand that having children would require a financial support system. So, they save and plan for future family in a mature way. Even so, you can't predict the potential downside of Family expenses if a child becomes sickly or any family member, particularly a parent, incurs a long-term illness.

Who you are, the current status of your Family lifecycle, and what role you play in your family will determine your Family Expenses. If you are single, then your "family" is you as the Inner Parent taking care of your Inner Child.

It's good to calculate these kinds of expenses as a family. At least spending money on self or family is somewhat satisfying. Paying money for work or debt obligations is much less so.

Family Expenses involve:

- Shelter
- Food
- Supplies
- School expenses
- Multiples of Personal Expenses
- All the physical, emotional, mental expenses for each child
- Etc.

SOCIAL AREAS OF YOUR LIFE

Your age determines the financial importance of your social life. As an individual, it's typically your teenage years up until you get married that your social life is the most important to you. However, as an adult you must also live somewhere, and this represents a social environment which has the potential to motivate your spending. Let's outline some various social areas where you might spend your money.

Money spent to be part of a group would be social. Clearly this involves such expenses as group fees when joining a club or organization, sporting equipment to participate as part of a team, travel expenses to partake in social adventures, meals and drinks involving social occasions such as birthday parties, holiday celebrations or high school reunions.

You might pay to join a ski club and then incur costs to go on trips during the year. If you do it because you like to ski, it's more personal. If you do it to hang out with the people you go with, it's more social. You can have more than one reason for spending money. Just be careful you aren't using a "good sounding" reason to justify the actual "bad sounding" reason.

Spending to impress others is social spending. You may incur social expenses trying to keep up with the Joneses in your neighborhood. Perhaps you want to project a lavish lifestyle beyond your means. You might buy pricy brand items for social approval even though the generic brand would do the job.

The clothes you buy, the car you drive, the vacations you pick could be an attempt to gain social acceptance. Thousand Oaks, CA, was a town known for people who would buy a partially constructed house they could ill afford. They would then finish and furnish only the downstairs and leave the upstairs completely raw and unfinished. They could entertain and put on a show, but no guest was allowed upstairs.

There could be a wide variety of reasons you spend in the social category. It only makes sense to evaluate your expenses based on this criterion when it does not specifically involve your Personal World, i.e. your physical, emotional or mental needs.

Social spending is theoretically discretionary spending, as opposed to something you actually require for your personal survival or work. Tabulating and evaluating your expenses in this lifestyle area will give you many clues for stretching and extending your hard-earned income.

Chapter 16: The Sinks: Money Action Accounts

Each month as part of the *Your Money or Your Life* system, you evaluate each of your expense categories. You decide for each category whether you spent about the right amount for this category, would like to spend less, or perhaps spend even more if spending in this category made you happy. This is an opportunity for both Inner Selves to communicate based on your conscious SELF-Parenting thoughts and discussions.

The money you spend and the lifestyle you live should reflect your personal values. This is basically the goal of spending money. The social areas of your life are typically where you have the most discretion to make personal choices that reflect who you are on the inside.

When money is tight you often don't have the option to cut spending in your personal or work areas. Ideally, your social time is your most pleasurable time. Yet you might find your social expenses putting a financial crimp on your Personal and Work lives. Truly all these details are up to your SELF-Parenting style and your personal situation. No one else can work this out for you.

Social Expenses take place in such areas as:

- Dining
- Dates
- Vacations
- Gifts/Flowers
- Vacations
- Clothes
- Hobbies
- Travel
- Vacations
- Fun
- Etc.

SELF-Parenting For LIFE:

WORK AREAS OF YOUR LIFE

Expenses in the work category are not necessarily money you spend at work or for work, unless you are a businessperson/entrepreneur. If you are in business for yourself, this puts you in the entrepreneurial Professional Relationship category which is outside the scope of this book.

The "work expenses" you have primarily relates to the money you spend as a result of your specific job and working life. The way to know if your expense is work-related is to ask yourself the following question. "Would I be spending this exact money if I didn't have this job?" If the only reason you are spending this money is because of your job, these are personal work expenses. And it's very unlikely you could deduct them come tax time.

Some examples of work expenses are travel costs that you would not have if you did not work where you do. Maybe your job requires you to maintain certain standards such as the clothing and wardrobe you must buy to represent your role at work. Perhaps you need to purchase a uniform or buy a specific category of shoes you would not personally wear to fit in with your work environment. Maybe as a teacher you are spending your own money on school supplies for your students. (which I applaud you for!)

Perhaps you've heard the saying that "time is money." This certainly applies to the travel time required back and forth to work at your present job. For example, what if it takes you one hour to get to work and one hour back? Then you need to divide your income for that day based on 10 hours of work instead of eight hours. Suddenly a ten dollar an hour job becomes an eight dollar an hour job when you add two extra hours of "unpaid work" traveling back and forth.

Chapter 16: The Sinks: Money Action Accounts

Once you start tracking your work expenses based on their time cost, the actual income from your job becomes more accurate. It might start to bug you that you are spending more time or money than you realized. These kinds of expenses can affect you in multiple ways.

Perhaps an increase in pay and a promotion puts you in a higher tax bracket with more stress which completely wipes out your current lifestyle. It is also possible that evaluating your current work expenses might reveal some financial blessings that previously you took for granted.

Evaluating your personal time and work expenses comes in handy if you are being offered a new job or position. Maybe this new role involves new travel requirements or relocating to a more expensive location. Are you going to need to spend more time and money at seminar weekends to upgrade your résumé?

Once you start using an accurate financial yardstick to evaluate these types of changes your two selves could determine that what looks like an opportunity might actually involve a downgrade of true income and/or lifestyle.

It's also possible that a potential job offer that looks lackluster at first might have some hidden advantages once projected changes in expenses and/or savings are considered. For the people whom work is the dominant factor in their lives, evaluating your complete spending related to a job can be an eye-opening and life changing experience.

Personal Work Expenses involve such things as:

- Clothes
- Travel
- Time
- Expensive and unhealthy meals
- Snacks
- Unreimbursed supplies
- Unreimbursed anything
- Etc.

PROFESSIONAL AREAS OF YOUR LIFE

There are two kinds of professional expenses. The ones we all must endure are those related to paying professionals for services we need for living life. These are costs such as going to the doctor, getting your car repaired and having your taxes done. These kinds of expenses are typically unavoidable in the modern world. Some of them can be extremely painful such as hiring a lawyer to fend off a spurious lawsuit or paying the fine for a ticket you didn't deserve.

The more complicated society becomes, the more services that were once free between family or friends have become professionalized. These include such expenses as eating out at restaurants instead of having dinners at home, paying to exercise instead of working out as part of a social group, or buying friends by joining expensive clubs or societies.

The second type of professional expense involves you as an entrepreneur or business owner. Here you have gone beyond "work." Now you are the professional in this relationship. Your expenses are part of doing business or providing your professional services. As mentioned, these are outside the scope of this book, so I won't discuss them further. If this is your situation there are many sources to help you in this area.

MANAGING MONEY EVEN HAS COSTS

Ouch! Spending money as a function of spending money seems to be hidden inside the activities related to money flow. The powers that be did a good job on this one.

Areas where you spend money related to Buying are:

- Time spent shopping
- Travel to stores, destinations.
- Financial fees
- Study/decision time.
- More Fees
- Planning
- Creating
- Research
- Etc.

Areas where you spend related to Selling are:

- PayPal's cut
- Writing checks
- Postage
- Financial fees
- Time spent: Admin hours.
- Time spent: Face time with buyers
- Advertising
- Answering the phone/emails
- Etc.

Even More Selling Expenses

- Time before and after
- More Travel
- Weekend Expos
- Professional Fees
- Planning costs
- Creating ads
- Printing
- Hiring professionals
- Seminars
- Various
- Etc.

Soon, we are going to look at the other Action Sink Account, that for Earning. There will be many key understandings about earning money from the SPP point of view.

But next, you are going to learn the Second Greatest SELF-Parenting tip for managing money. It's even better and more powerful than the first one if such a thing is possible. It even gets its own chapter and it's something you can (and should, dare I say must) start immediately if you want to conquer money.

Chapter 17:

The Second-Best Self-Parenting Money Tip of All Time

Chapter 17: The Second-Best SELF-Parenting Money Tip of All Time

Here's your second truly awesome SELF-Parenting tip for living in your Financial World. This is a time-honored principle of money management. Although not new, it may be new to you if you haven't heard it before. This idea is based on the familiar concept of tithing. Many religions use tithing as a way for you to contribute to their well-being. Giving 10% of your income to your place of worship is the normal use of the word tithing.

In the SELF-Parenting form of tithing we take a different approach. As the Inner Parent, you are going to take ten percent of any money both selves earn and place it directly under your Inner Child's control by creating what we call a money magnet.

Ten percent of any new income is paid directly to your Inner Child, before any other expenses. Why is this a good idea? So many reasons!

- You've just spent some of your earnings which are now "gone," as in no longer available for other expenses. This prevents you from spending it elsewhere.
- You have just created a "savings account" in your Inner Child's name, which will become a formidable asset and the bottom layer of your Asset Bathtub.
- You have energized your Inner Child to experience something new. Now, instead of all your money being gone and having nothing to show for it, your IC has its own money.
- This inspires the energy (magnetic-electrical powers) of your Inner Child to create more earnings so it can add to its Money Magnet.

Whatever amount you make, it's easy to calculate 10% and "pay your Inner Child first." All you do is move the decimal point over to the left one slot. The amount of 234.65 becomes 23.46, etc. As soon as your income comes in, you place the money in your Money Magnet and then you forget about it. People who do this say that it's very easy to pay this money first, and they don't even miss it as the rest of their week/month continues.

Because it's your Inner Child's money, s/he feels good about having something of its own. The key to this idea is to keep it in real currency, not a check or a fake coupon. Ideally, your Money Magnet is kept as close to your physical person as possible in your house or apt. You don't put this money in the bank unless it becomes a sum so large your Inner Child becomes worried that it will get taken or lost somehow.

This money truly does act like a money magnet. Your Inner Child is the emotional energetic one. It's now getting the concept that whatever money the two of you earn, it gets to keep 10%. If you find a dime on the street, a penny goes in your Money Magnet. When your paycheck arrives, 10% in cash is immediately transferred and then it's forgotten about, as you live on the rest. Once this becomes a habit your spending patterns essentially remain the same. Only now, you have this glowing ember of magnetic power motivating your Inner Child to earn more.

Here's the trick, you never spend your Money Magnet, ever! You let it accumulate and as it does, your Inner Child feels the value and strength of having such an asset. You never spend the Money Magnet! This is the Inner Child's Money Magnet! Not yours! If it goes away, your Inner Child is going to lose motivated to make any more and you don't want to feel this pain. Earning money is hard enough.

Here's another trick about the Money Magnet. You don't put it in the bank. If you do it becomes the bank's Money Magnet. Wherever the money is stored, it pulls, attracts, and magnetizes that place for more money to join it. So, you need to keep your

Chapter 17: The Second-Best SELF-Parenting Money Tip of All Time

Money Magnet near you in a safe place which your Inner Child approves. That way if your Inner Child wants to count and play with the money, it can. Clearly you want to keep this money in a safe place based on your current living situation.

If you live alone, easily done. You can find a home location that only you know about. If you live with roommates for example, you'll have to be more discrete and find a safe place to secure your cash that only you know about. You just need to keep it safe and nearby so that your Inner Child has easy access to it. Your IC also needs to rely on you, the Inner Parent, not to throw this money away on something else.

Also, as part of this action, you don't tell anyone else about your Money Magnet. Why would you? It doesn't affect them and it's none of their business anyway. If you don't tell anybody about it, then no one can go looking for it. This is a private matter strictly between you and your Inner Child.

As your pennies turn into dollars keeping your Money Magnet in an envelope is fine. When tens and twenties accumulate, you can swap them for hundreds. You can use a bank bottle with a coin deposit on the top that keeps track of the amount of inserted coins. This is very handy. Keep the bills in an envelope and the coins in the coin bank so it's easy to count and keep track of.

Know that your Inner Child is going to love counting and keeping track of its Money Magnet as it grows. This is his/her money and is never going to go anywhere. If you must put it in a bank for whatever reason, make sure that your Inner Child oversees the paperwork and knows that this money is completely under its control.

In the "olden days" there was an excellent choice when you got a little passbook at the bank with your deposits written in it. Your IC could go to the bank, make the MM deposit with the passbook, and then keep it close, maybe even under its pillow or mattress. All those deposits would add up to a tidy sum and it was very satisfying to watch it grow. Plus, it was safe.

If you are more on the poor side, this could seem like a difficult thing to ask. But once you start keeping a Money Magnet suddenly you find it's just as easy to live on the remaining money as you did before. This is one of the beauties of the Money Magnet in that your unconscious spending becomes naturally reduced.

Even if you continue spending unconsciously for a while, since you already have intentionally put 10% aside, it's "okay" to just keep spending the way you normally do. You'll have slightly less (only 10%), but in the back of your mind, your Inner Child knows that it has a growing sum money acting as an unconscious magnet to pull in more.

Starting your Money Magnet when you are poor is the best time and the best way to become the master of your Financial World. Learning and practicing this tithing skill while earning only pennies and dollars, becomes the fun and mental foundation for your ongoing success. Soon your Inner Child and your Money Magnet will begin pulling in tens, and thousands, and perhaps even millions.

If you are more in the average income category, then your Money Magnet can start accumulating quickly. At the end of 3-6 months, you might find that you have a rather tidy sum in that sock, or coffee can, or wherever you keep your Money Magnet.

Chapter 17: The Second-Best SELF-Parenting Money Tip of All Time

However, you can't spend it. Don't even think about it. Not for any reason. Not taxes, vacation, food, nada. As far as money you can spend, it's already spent, it's in your Money Magnet.

If you need more money for something, go out an earn it, using your current Money Magnet to attract and pull in more money.

Another advantage of the Money Magnet is that once you see that you really can "save money" then you can begin paying money into some other accounts for which you would like to save or make payments. Just set these up after you have your Money Magnet working for at least three months.

You don't want to set up a bunch of new savings accounts until your Money Magnet is a solid habit. Creating several extra saving accounts through over excitement could make it so you really do become low on money. Just put 10% aside, and let your life continue as is until your Money Magnet becomes a done deal.

Once you are ready, try planning some kind of other account as a test. Let's say you'd like to take a vacation next year. Start putting a percent of new money into that account, maybe 5%. If some financial crisis arises, you can use that money. After all, it was just there for a proposed vacation which was optional. Maybe you would even spend that money on something else once you had enough to take that vacation. It might not seem like such a great idea anymore.

If you know you must pay 20% of your income to taxes, you should already have a tax account where you put 20% of what you earn. Just know to pay your Money Magnet first. This is the one primary account that matters in your life. Take another 20% and put it into your tax account. Don't worry, the numbers will work out in the end.

Tax money is gone from your life. Your Money Magnet will continue to magnetize and pull new money into your life. Pay yourself first so your Inner Child becomes motivated to energize ways to manifest future income.

If your paycheck already has money taxes taken out, then perfect. Just put 10% of that amount into your Money Magnet. Do this with hard currency. Don't use a check for the amount in the can. It needs to be real money that your Inner Child can see and count. If you are so lucky as to get a tax return at the end of the year, that's right, 10% goes into your Money Magnet. It's new money, so in it goes.

Don't round up or down on the amount. The percent is ten. If your paycheck is $867.32, then you need to put 86 dollars and 73 cents into your money magnet. Any new money that comes into your life as new income has 10% of that amount immediately subtracted and placed into your Money Magnet. Your Inner Child will actually thrill to this experience as you continue to do this over time.

If your income is deposited directly into your bank, then you need to make a separate exact 10% cash withdrawal to put in your Money Magnet. Again, this needs to be real money, money your Inner Child can touch and witness. And never borrow from your Money Magnet. This is not good. Your Inner Child can be a very bad lender.

If you need to borrow money for some reason from an outside source, this does not go into your Money Magnet. That's already a liability. Also, if you sell an asset for less money than you paid, don't put 10% in because it's not "new money." If you made profit on the sale, then add 10% to reflect the new money portion.

Chapter 17: The Second-Best SELF-Parenting Money Tip of All Time

If you somehow enter the unfortunate circumstances of borrowing money to live, keep your Money Magnet outside this process as long as you can. Your Money Magnet is the magnetic source of your future income. You can trust me that if you start keeping a Money Magnet your borrowing days will soon be over. If you borrow from your money magnet, you are doomed.

As your Money Magnet accumulates, your Inner Parent may be tempted now and then to spend it. Let's say you have accumulated over $4000 in your money magnet. Wow, that could be used for _____, says the Inner Parent. No! Not even. That's your Inner Child's money and needs to remain exactly where it is so your Inner Child can earn another 40,000 to make the new money magnet number $8000.

Thus, another side benefit of the Money Magnet. Whatever amount is in there means you earned that amount with two zeros added. This can be very eye opening for both inner selves. It begins to make the earning power of your Money Magnet very real.

Even if you make a huge salary, all your life it can feel like you've been poor when you have nothing in your pockets. Suddenly you now have $22,216.22 dollars in your Money Magnet. This means you have earned $222,162.20 over that period, even though you spent it all and don't have a dime as usual.

Before your Money Magnet you truly would have nothing to show for it. You might not even have realized that two hundred and twenty-two thousand, one hundred and sixty-two dollars went through your fingers during these last three days/weeks/months/years.

Even now, you the Inner Parent have nothing to show for it; your wallet is empty. You've spent all your money. But your

Inner Child knows about the $22,216.22 in its Money Magnet. It knows its role is to magnetize your life and energy to make more.

Along the way, your Inner Parent is going to develop the understanding that if you don't have the money, you can't spend it on some non-essential expenditure. If you don't have the money, you can't buy that thing, whatever it is your Inner Parent wants. If you want it really, really bad, then earn more money, budget for the expense, and be a good Inner Parent.

If you want some expensive "thing/trip/experience" and you think the Money Magnet is your answer, no, it's not. Whatever you truly desire, earn the money for it, and in the meantime, you'll be contributing more to your Money Magnet as a side benefit. Your Inner Child's electricity is the energy that runs this motor. Whatever scale of your earning, small or large, your Money Magnet will enhance your Financial World.

If you spend your Inner Child's Money Magnet, for whatever reason, you'll find yourself bereft of energy to earn anything more once it's gone. That motorcycle you want so bad can crash or be stolen. That vacation with your friend will be over the second you spend your Money Magnet for the deposit.

If you don't have the money for whatever you want to do, thinking your Money Magnet might be the source, no, you don't have the money and no, you can't do it. Don't learn the hard way what it's like to accumulate a tidy sum in your Money Magnet and then fritter it away instantly on something that turns out to be useless.

If you can manage only one financial account and do it properly, your Money Magnet is by far the most important account to manage. Your skills in your Financial World and

Chapter 17: The Second-Best SELF-Parenting Money Tip of All Time

determination with your Money Magnet will give your Inner Parent the clarity and experience to understand more complicated financial activities such as paying bills, earning a living, and providing for your eventual retirement years. Your Money Magnet, starting as of right now, will be the seed that becomes the root that grows your money-making tree. Maybe money can grow on trees.

Chapter 18:

You Have Your Money Magnet, Now What?

Chapter 18: You Have Your Money Magnet, Now What?

Okay, your Money Magnet is in place and rocking your Financial World. Now what?

You have bills to pay, that's what. In the Bathtub/Sinks System think of any money that you spend as a bill, expense, cash out of your life, bye-bye; even though this might not exactly be the case based on the principles of double entry bookkeeping. Essentially a financially successful day, week, month is one where you spend less money than you earn.

The Bathtubs/Sinks System gives you four accounts to deal with. Two are action accounts and two are repository accounts. The goal is to be proactive about your sink activities by paying your (daily, weekly, monthly) expenses with income. And you can earn as much extra income as you need to be happy.

Your action accounts are Spending and Earning. You spend or earn in your sinks, and the tabulated results flow directly into your assets and liabilities bathtubs where they relax and settle on their own.

You have many motivations for spending money. The purpose of your spending ultimately determines the account under which it is classified. You could spend money on food for physical, emotional, or mental reasons; as well as family, social, or work reasons. Whatever the ultimate logic you have for your food purchase, ultimately, it's still going to be money (an asset) spent paying for an expense (food).

Think of spending your money as "gone." You had money but now you don't. You spend money based on one of three actions. Here is where the rules of the Bathtub/Sinks Money game get down to the nitty gritty reality of your Financial World.

- You spend money on Monthly Living Expenses.
- You spend money to lower a liability.
- You spend money for, or to increase, an asset.

Basically, in the Bathtub/Sinks System anything that is not an asset is deemed a liability. In the "real world" of Double Entry Bookkeeping there are more traditional designations of asset and liability categories. But for right now, this is about your SELF-Parenting decisions, and how you and your Inner Child energize your sink spending activities.

Money spent on food could be deemed an asset if it was eaten and you derived pleasure from it. Money spent on food could be a liability if you didn't eat it, it made you sick, or it was primarily to create a mood such as getting drunk or high. Even so, if you deem getting drunk or high an asset for you, that's okay in your mind.

The bottom line? Any money you spend on food is gone from your life. It's no longer a liquid asset you can use for another purpose. If it was junk food making your body sicker and more miserable then it's a double liability. Call it a triple liability if you used an over-extended credit card to pay for it.

From a SELF-Parenting point of view, if you look at all the spending you make listed in a row, you could give each transaction a designation of asset or liability. Only you can make this determination. If you are spending money on a doughnut and coffee, and that's an asset to you, then it's goes in the asset column. If you consider this a bad choice, but you do it anyway, it goes into the liability column.

Either way in the "real world" when you spend your money on food, that money is gone. You no longer have it to spend on

Chapter 18: You Have Your Money Magnet, Now What?

anything else, so it becomes an expense in the Bathtub/Sinks System.

If you spend your money on car insurance, it's also gone. It goes towards an expense called insurance which is a reality of life. Actually, insurance could be deemed an asset because it protects you and others if anything bad happens involving your automobile. It is a gamble you must take whether it pays off or not and truly you don't really want it to pay off anyway. However, once the money is spent, it's gone, so it's liability from your sink point of view.

Technically a single financial transaction can cover different purposes. For example, if you are spending 400 a month for a car loan, technically at least three transactions are taking place:

- You are paying down a liability (the loan on the car).
- You are increasing an asset (you own more of the car).
- A percentage of the money goes to interest for the privilege of borrowing.

In whatever way you count it and no matter which category an accountant would give it, the Bathtub/Sinks System says your money is gone the second you spend it. You just don't have it anymore to spend anywhere else. Plus, even though your car is an asset to you, it's going to be worth less over time; so, it truly is "gone money." Eventually you will not own that car.

From this perspective, even your money magnet tithing is an expense; it's gone. You can't access or spend it, other than to admire and feel proud about it as your Inner Child pulls in more income for you.

In your life when employing the Bathtub/Sinks System, think of all your spending as gone money. Your Inner Child can certainly understand this perspective.

Knowing your expenses is WAY better than not knowing your expenses. This is where keeping track of every penny in and out of your life is going to be so amazing. This will be true even if you hate money, can't stand financial responsibility, or don't like anything to do with numbers.

It's better to know (and cry if you have to) where your hard-earned money goes during the month. Being in denial, not knowing, or ignoring or bluffing your way through your Financial World is the unconscious way you were before SELF-Parenting.

Month to month is the best way to evaluate your spending patterns. The fixed expenses that most of us have typically repeat every month. If there is something you need to buy once a year, say car insurance, then you simply divide this by 12 and put it into the monthly spending.

If you have seasonal expenses such as buying heating oil only in the winter, take last year's total and divide this number into twelve monthly chunks. This is an excellent way for both inner selves to keep an eye on spending, even if it's not winter. Maybe your summer money is looking good and you want to spend some, until you realize that come the fall you're going to need that exact money for a winter expense.

The ideal in your Financial World is to never be surprised by some category of spending, that would not truly surprise someone with more financial savvy. Assuming you have a stable living situation, after a few years following these tips, you will have an accurate and complete picture of what you spend on

Chapter 18: You Have Your Money Magnet, Now What?

"fixed" expenses during the year. If you know you are going to buy a new pair of shoes every year, even this would be accounted for in your budget.

LET'S TALK ABOUT BUDGETS

A budget is nothing more than an estimated total of your expenses that you have each month. You will certainly have ongoing expenses that occur month after month. Once you total them you get a number and that number is an excellent way for you, as a smart SELF-Parenting practitioner, to be aware in a "light way" of where your money goes each month.

For some people, a budget sounds negative. It sounds like something that mandates what you can spend. Maybe they had to adhere to a strict budget at a job and there was never enough money allocated to the proper categories. This is not the case with your budget. Your budget is perfect and will never cause you a problem because you are making it and it reflects your life, and your life only.

Your budget is your estimated, normal living expenses in your life, today, based on the reality of what your two inner selves do every day. Once you have genuine figures and they accurately reflect your spending, you can use this knowledge to plan whatever improvements you seek in your Financial World. In fact, think of your budget as "last month's spending." It's what you truly spent, not some rule-bound system you must adhere to.

For you, the SELF-Parenting practitioner, your budget is a guide, like a map, that shows the journey of your money through the month. Use it to plan and estimate your current spending patterns, based on what is typical, so you can concentrate on other important life concerns that have nothing to do with money.

Assuming you enjoy a comfortable income and know your spending patterns, the average of 3-6 months spending will be a fair approximation of how much money it takes to live your life each month. Once you know your true monthly outgo, you can plan with more certainty. There are two ways to "beat your budget" if it's not where you would like to be:

- Spend less than expected, or
- Earn more than expected.

If you find out, based on your calculations, that you are spending more money than you make, then you have an immediate need to lower your spending or increase your income. Don't think this couldn't happen. Many SELF-Parenting practitioners have been extremely unhappy to learn that this is indeed what was happening with their money.

If you have never truly taken a serious look at your finances before, you can use your new-found knowledge to consider the real numbers of your sink spending and plan to make changes that will benefit both selves in the long run.

For example, starting your Money Magnet is guaranteed to benefit you in the long run. You are basically creating a saving account, also known as a hard asset. Yet, you also will never spend it. Even though the money is "psychologically gone" the fact that your Inner Child has a Money Magnet means you will be attracting more money to you. It truly is an asset in the long term as it remains with you physically forever.

As you become more familiar with your deepest spending patterns, you will learn how to navigate the complex world of

Chapter 18: You Have Your Money Magnet, Now What?

managing your money. This pattern resides deep within your SELF-Parenting Style. When you get to the point in time when you can shed light in this area with your daily SELF-Parenting sessions, you will have become an experienced practitioner indeed. This is the SELF-Parenting big leagues as far as awareness goes.

Chapter 19:

The Earning Sink: Money Coming In

Chapter 19: The Earning Sink: Money Coming In

Typically, as an adult entering society you will need to start earning money to survive. Otherwise you'll find out that people get mad at you and eventually you find yourself out on the street.

How you earn money is up to you. Ideally, it will be doing something you enjoy. Perhaps you are lucky enough to be involved with a family business, or maybe you don't consider this lucky. Typically, people do something called "getting a job." Depending on your current age and social environment, by the time you are reading this book you may have had extensive experiences in this area.

Most SELF-Parenting practitioners need to start earning money at some point. Given this obvious necessity, the easiest thus best way to earn money is by doing something your Inner Child enjoys. The reason might not jump out at you right away.

To earn enough money, you typically need to work a lot of hours. When "work" is something your Inner Child enjoys, you don't even consider this work. You may have read the profile of some rich/famous person who says, "I can't believe I get paid for doing what I love..." This is a nice experience and a goal you can achieve. I have.

Ideally, you begin to explore your Financial World in partnership with your Inner Child early in your career. Some people unconsciously self-parent themselves into a job/career that their Inner Child finds distasteful even though it was promised to offer more money.

First of all, the expected money may never even happen. The industry can change on a dime. The projected market may fail to meet expectations. Something else happened that nobody could predict, thus the big money never shows.

Even if it does these people often pay a price for the money that does come through. There are too many stories of people who became a doctor or a lawyer because that's what pleased their parents, or because they thought that would be the best way to make "a lot of" money. Only after they invested all the time and money to reach this false goal (for them) did they realize (maybe even both IP and IC) they had zero interest in doctoring or lawyering.

It's an important aspect of your conscious SELF-Parenting that you dialog with your Inner Child to learn which areas of life in which s/he would like to earn money. This is an ongoing lifetime process.

When you first begin earning you may have limited options and opportunities to make money. But certainly, your Inner Child has opinions about what it does and doesn't like to do. And there are opportunities to make money in just about any area of life. Simply start with your purpose and see where you end up.

Following your Inner Child's dreams is an excellent place to start. Just taking the first steps to follow your dreams will make you happy as soon as you begin. Achieving genuine dreams will bring true satisfaction. Going for some external Inner Parent ego fantasy just because it looks good is like attempting to eat waxed fruit.

One way to think about earning money as far as jobs go, is to consider the three categories of work loosely categorized as:

1. A Job
2. A Career
3. A Calling

Chapter 19: The Earning Sink: Money Coming In

A job is basically just a way for you to make money. This is completely fine, if the limits of what you are looking for is only to make money, then any job you are happy doing will fit the bill.

You are probably getting your fulfillment in life from activities outside of work, such as your personal, family, or social life. You are happy to put in hours working because you know and agree that this is what you have to do. But you look forward to time off and don't think much about your job when you aren't working.

A career becomes something you could actually see yourself doing for a longer period, perhaps the rest of your life. Maybe you enjoy working in this area and you are motivated by and see a path for advancement over time.

A career may align with your studies or perhaps you just fell into this line of work as a job, but now you like it, or the people, or the benefits it provides. The daily grind is okay if not invigorating. Your daily activities fit with your self-esteem and it seems to go along with your needs on a longer-term basis.

A calling would be the ideal way that most of us earned money if such a thing was possible. Our motivation for this type of work goes beyond any thoughts of money. We are in this area of work to serve others, make new discoveries, create a better world or pursue a goal we feel passionate about. Maybe all of the above. When work is a calling we are motivated by a higher purpose. It may be hard, but it doesn't feel like work. We enjoy the challenge and the rewards if our calling is fulfilled.

It's probably a good idea to note that none of these choices might last forever. Given the fast pace of modern life and all the ways that our best laid plans can go awry, it's just not possible to be certain that we could remain working at the same job/career/calling for our entire working career.

Even if you start with your true calling, in ten years the whole industry might change and completely ruin why it was a calling for you. You can move, get married/divorced, other life events can happen that throw you for a loop. So, it's important that within your SELF-Parenting Style you remain flexible and open to the twists and turns your life may take.

There are multiple ways your IC or IP could demonstrate s/he does not like a specific job, career, or your choice for a calling. These symptoms may appear in your Personal or Relational Worlds even though they are caused by your Financial World endeavors. They take the form of niggling inner conflicts that start creating symptoms that eat away at your mind, your energy levels, and your daily enjoyment of life.

Some examples are frequent headaches, being tired all the time, needing stimulants to get through your day and downers to sleep at night, expensive toys or exotic vacations to make your suffering "worth it." There could be a multitude of mysterious physical, emotional, and mental symptoms you might never have if you weren't involved in your current work situation.

It's up to your Inner Parent to be vigilant about what these nonfinancial "costs" might be and include them in your Financial World calculations. If you didn't have distasteful working conditions, perhaps your normal life would be better than your fantasy vacation.

Early adulthood typically involves various experiments such as trying different jobs to see how you like them. Maybe you were forced by poverty to take a job you thought you would hate but you wound up loving it. The opposite could happen. Somehow

Chapter 19: The Earning Sink: Money Coming In

you luck into what you thought would be your ideal job only to find it becomes a painful ordeal after a while.

Maybe your job is loved by your Inner Parent but disliked by your Inner Child; or vice versa. These are the types of SELF-Parenting explorations for which you must stay flexible and work out any inner conflicts between you and your Inner Child. It's your job, your life. Everybody is different.

Maybe you are advanced in years and technology has passed you by. Whatever you were good at no longer has value like it once did. You were trained how to make buggy whips, but they just don't sell like they used to. Perhaps injuries or accidents have left you with difficult physical symptoms that hold you back. Conceivably you've found yourself needing to support other people through no fault of your own. What can you do to lighten your expenses and transition to more fulfilling circumstances?

Typically, there is a strong desire on your Inner Child's side to follow a certain direction or pursuit. You need to be aware of this as the Inner Parent and structure life opportunities that support your Inner Child's dreams and desires. This is because your Inner Child is the original energy source for living/working. If s/he doesn't like what you are doing s/he will simply stop providing energy. Then you can forget about enjoying work or play!

Look for a purpose both your Inner Child and Inner Parent find fulfilling. It's easier to accept low pay or terrible working conditions (for a while) if you know they are part of breaking into the big time. Being a waiter is a time-honored path to seeking Hollywood fame and fortune. But you'd better move to NY or LA, not remain a lowly waiter in Des Moines hoping to be discovered somehow. To enter a high-profile profession, you must often prove your worth and staying power, called "paying your dues."

On a recent Saturday night, I spent all evening until late the next day shuffling papers and writing notes from an event I went to that day. It was very mundane, chasing down numbers, making copies from copies, and in general doing nothing of any value except straightening stuff out.

But I enjoyed it to the max. I really accomplished something because I was motivated by starting a new business and learning as I went. I was building a cathedral if you know this analogy.

I made zero money with these activities, but it was all about my Financial World. My Inner Child was the source of my happiness and as the Inner Parent I went along for the ride. It was a win/win Financial World venture that involved no money at all.

INCOME

How much money do you make an hour, day, week, month? Do you have a steady job with a set paycheck? Or are you living hand to mouth, scraping for every penny. One good thing about the Bathtubs/Sinks Theory accounting system is that every penny you make goes into the asset bathtub. Assuming you earn more than you spend, you will have a positive income. If you spend more than you earn, some changes will need to be made.

Since there are so many ways of earning money, you will have to draw your own list that reflects your life. Perhaps you have a set job, and that's the only money coming in. Or maybe you have three jobs, or you sell things that you make, or have services that you render. As you keep a running total of these sums

Chapter 19: The Earning Sink: Money Coming In

from your various income accounts you can compare them from month to month.

Perhaps you'll discover that you make pretty good money doing something you enjoy, but you don't spend that many hours doing it for some reason. If you can rearrange your schedule to put more hours into that activity, not only will you enjoy these hours more, more money naturally follows.

RULES OF THE BATHTUB/SINK MONEY GAME

- The first rule for your Financial World is to make more money each month than you spend. This is goal number one.
- The second rule is to spend money in the best way possible, by maximizing the value you receive from the hours you spend making it.
- The third rule is to plan your financial world so perfectly, that you become free of money concerns using the money you earn and accumulate to pursue Personal and Relationship goals.

The current key for you, whatever your circumstances, is to apply your conscious SELF-Parenting Style to improve your income assuming you would like more money in your life. *Your Money or Your Life,* will guide you over the long term to keep moving toward the fulfillment of your financial goals.

If you don't currently have a job or you would like to explore other opportunities or professions, I have another book to recommend. I'm not going to make a whole chapter out of it like the other books. It's very well-known and has been around for years. If you are looking for a job or a career change, it's filled with quality advice.

SELF-Parenting For LIFE:

Third Most Amazing Money Tip

For evaluating careers, I like a book called, *What Color Is Your Parachute*. I've read this book several times and I still don't know why it has this title, but I can tell you it's filled with excellent actionable suggestions for improving your financial happiness. If you are unhappy at your current job it will guide you towards finding work that correlates with your purpose, ideals and talents. It has so many ideas you may even find your calling.

It's one of those books that is edited and evolves on a yearly basis, and the last edition I read, I liked it even more. Like *Your Money or Your Life*, if you want to earn more income or switch careers, you just need to get this book. Read it carefully and do whatever it says based on your IP/IC negotiations. From this point-of-view it's like one long SELF-Parenting Module.

What you do to earn money is potentially the most intimate part of you. It's likely the most hours you spend during the day. By default, it is your service to humanity. Or perhaps you need to do anything you can just to survive. Each person's life is individual in this way.

I can tell you that your SELF-Parenting Style is the key to this area. If you are making money in some way that makes your Inner Child unhappy, then this is bad, very bad. It's up to your Inner Parent to investigate this fully and do what you can to help your Inner Child to a Win/Win outcome.

However, this can be tricky. You just can't quit a job your Inner Child hates, if it's your only means of survival, especially if you have a family to care for. You must use your SELF-Parenting skills, and a book such as *What Color Is Your Parachute*, to explore your options given your current situation. Many people have completely turned around their life circumstances through positive SELF-Parenting using the tactics in *What Color Is Your Parachute*.

One strategy that has been around for a while is to turn a beloved hobby into a money-making endeavor. This is an internet favorite and there are many ideas for this on YouTube. Just search your hobby and making money. There will be many examples for you to view. Just be careful not to get sucked into some new way of spending money.

Another money saving idea is to move to a less expensive city, state, or country with a skill set that would be valued. These kinds of strategies have been explored quite extensively in the past 20 years with advent of the internet and increasing globalization. I probably don't have any breakthrough ideas you haven't heard already.

Your Financial World is the final of the three worlds for living your life that is your responsibility and yours only, so take heed. If you weren't already consciously aware of these strategies, engage your positive SELF-Parenting Style to dig in and fast-track your financial well-being.

Chapter 20:
A Brief Introduction to Generic Human Studies (GHS)

Chapter 20: A Brief Introduction to Generic Human Studies (GHS)

This book has been written through the lens of the SELF-Parenting Program for the purpose of providing a deeper understanding into the bigger picture of Generic Human Studies. GHS is a philosophy that places each individual within the center of his/her own personal world. As a SELF-Parenting practitioner, you enjoy a unique practice that can lead directly to the deeper levels of GHS.

Generic Human Studies places YOU, as a unique instance of a human being, deep inside your three Worlds as introduced in prior chapters. Each person lives a self-interested life who's center falls in the middle of these three worlds. GHS discusses the big picture of human experience from within a body of knowledge that applies directly to each person.

GHS invites you to use your natural in-built motivation and experiences to learn and understand where and how you fit into the Generic Human Studies paradigm.

There's a book on this topic which explains GHS in full detail, called *What Is Generic Human Studies?* It's written as a set of questions that lead the reader gently through the system.

Below are just a few benefits of Generic Human Studies that make it worth your time to explore. When GHS becomes a shared reality with others it has several benefits. For example, GHS delivers the following features:

- Provides answers to questions other systems don't even know yet to ask.
- Solves problems other systems don't even know exist.
- Gives each human an easy mental smart system to explain the core of human experience.
- Is defined by generic principles that apply to all humans from every culture.

SELF-Parenting For LIFE:

- Provides life explanations that are easy to communicate to other people even if they don't know the system.
- Defines the areas of life where you have complete jurisdiction to create the life you desire.
- Defines the areas of life where you must cooperate with others to achieve life goals such as in relational and financial transactions.
- Eliminates difficult words and concepts so that even young children can understand the system.
- Unites all methods of healing under one paradigm so humanity can concentrate and improve every healing system.
- Reduces unneeded complexity and explains complicated non-generic systems using standard terms.
- Is concerned with individual humans, so it doesn't overreach or complicate other areas, such as politics, religion, or government.
- Models human experience based on third-party verifiable principles and is therefore consistent and reproducible.

Here's just one example of how amazing GHS can be. I've explained all the relevant areas of life you need to understand and work with as a SELF-Parenting Practitioner and yet, I mentioned Generic Human Studies hardly at all. Nonetheless you understand everything I've been saying so far correct? It just so happens that it all originated from within the GHS framework.

Here's another principle from Generic Human Studies for your consideration. Basically, if you have a problem, you'd like it solved, correct? You want it to go away? Am I right?

"Problem, problem go away;
come again no other day."

Chapter 20: A Brief Introduction to Generic Human Studies (GHS)

To live a life without problems seems pretty much impossible on the personal level. For the typical person reading this book, you probably have at least a few major problems that you'd like answers to if possible. And the less energy and effort required by you to solve a problem the better.

Let's start with this idea. Suppose you have 100 problems in your life. How can Generic Human Studies help you, even if you are not a practitioner of SELF-Parenting? Would reducing 100 problems down to about 20 be a good thing? If you could solve 80% of your true problems quickly without much effort does this sound attractive?

THE GHS PROMISE:

The GHS promise says that typically you can solve 80% of your true problems with 20% of your effort once you truly define what the problem is. Once understood if your problem is generic, it already has a generic solution. If so, just do that; problem solved!

If you could solve 80% of your life's problems with 20% of your effort are you willing to sign up for that deal? If 80% of your problems went away, do you think you might feel better about life?

Of course, you may then be left with what we call the "hard 20%," which to solve properly could take up to 80% of your time. But it's fun so you will enjoy it. After this you can go on a permanent vacation.

Here's another subtle but very powerful aspect of GHS problem-solving. Maybe you only have one problem in your life, but it's a truly bad one. How would you like an improved "solutional outcome" to your problem? What is a solutional outcome? It is the percent better your problem/situation/objective can improve, even if it's not 100% fixed.

Let's say you have a very bad situation. With GHS, it may not be completely correctable, but it could become 60% better. You should be happy about this. It's similar to this idea.

Let's say your goal is to make a million dollars but try as you may, you "only" make $600,000. That's still a pretty good "solutional outcome." Let's say every day you get punched in the face 100 times. If you can figure out a way to get punched in the face only 20 times a day, you'll be plenty pleased. You might even experience supreme happiness getting punched in the face only 20 times a day.

With GHS, all your solutional outcomes can improve, which many people don't even contemplate, much less consciously consider when going through their own life experiences.

How Can Generic Human Studies Work So Well?

These may sound like big promises, but there's a lot of history to back up these claims. It's easier to experience than to explain, but here is a try. For starters, most people don't even know about the Generic Human Studies system of problem evaluation. If they did, they wouldn't have 80% of the problems they have now. Once they learn it, their problems begin melting away never to return.

If you don't apply Generic Human Studies to your problem, you'll never know if it's going to work or not. First, you need to learn that GHS exists. Then you need to give it a trial test on a problem in your life.

Chapter 20: A Brief Introduction to Generic Human Studies (GHS)

Only then will you know how well it's going to work for you. This leads to an even deeper issue at hand that explains why people have so many problems in the first place.

People don't know what they don't know. This is an unfortunate circumstance for a few reasons. If people don't know what they don't know, they won't look for available options that could benefit them immensely.

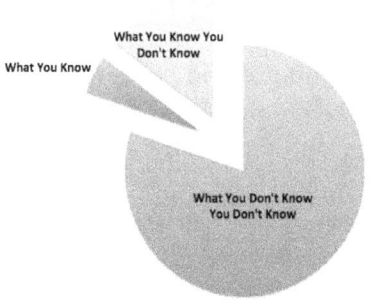

For most people it takes a severe problem to motivate them to seek a new idea or solution. Relatively happy people are often satisfied to remain grossly uninformed about things they don't know, even if these new teachings will help them in a big way.

Some people simply resist learning anything new for whatever reason. They can even be opposed to a new idea simply because they never heard it before.

How can you consider, contemplate, or make a decision about something you don't even know exists? How can you fix a problem you don't know you have? If you have a problem which you don't even know about, this is a problem right there.

If you don't know about GHS, then you don't know what you don't know. And in your specific situation, that's a problem that can easily bring you trouble you don't want. One easy example might be having a leak in your roof of which you are unaware. If it never rains, it may never become a problem.

When might you learn that you have a small leak in your roof? When it rains of course. And how easy will that problem be to fix when it's raining?

Once it stops raining, you could even forget about this problem for a time or two. Out of sight, out of mind. Why bother if it's not raining? Assuming you understand the concept that having a roof that doesn't leak is a good idea, only when you find out about it, can you make plans to repair it. Even then you might need a push.

Another aspect of not knowing what you don't know is that often the person with a problem can't see the problem even if everyone else can. For whatever reason, they don't see their own problem.

And, the ideal solution to this exact problem could be sitting right in front of their face. But since this mythical person is unaware a problem exists; they aren't seeking a solution. What's in front of his/her face might seem like an irritation instead of their next step into the infinite.

And here is an idea for you. If you aren't stepping into unlimited joy with infinite wonder every move you make, you may have a problem.

Chapter 21:
The Nine Words of Generic Human Studies

Chapter 21: The Nine Words of Generic Human Studies

Everything in your entire life that matters to you can be easily categorized using just one of nine words. Being able to place any potential problem into its correct category is the first and most important step towards solving your problem.

Where you think or assume a problem might be in your life, may not be where it truly exists at all. This is part of your reason problems aren't resolved.

You need to accurately define the true category for each problem that you are experiencing. Defining your problem accurately is the first step for problem solving.

To do this we use what are called the Nine Words of Generic Human Studies. These nine words are already familiar to you as they have been used throughout the book. They are:

For a Personal Problem:

- Physical
- Emotional
- Mental

For a Relational Problem:

- Family
- Social
- Work

For a Financial Problem:

- Expense
- Income
- Transfer

All you do is assign your problem to its correct category of transaction remembering these three points.

- Personal means that no other person involved
- Relational means you are on a relationship seesaw with one other person
- Financial means it involves money as your primary focus

If you are having trouble accurately assigning one of your problems to a category, then ask someone else. Often, they can easily tell you which category of problem you have, because they aren't the one with this problem.

Here's an idea to focus your thoughts. Write down as many problems as you can think of. List them on a page. Assign them a category based on the Nine Words of Generic Human Studies.

Here's some simple examples: Nine Word

- You feel bad   Physical
- You feel sad   Emotional
- You feel mad   Mental
- Something is not going well
  with a Family Member   Family
- Something is not going well with a
  Social Relationship   Social
- Something is not going well with a
  Work Relationship   Work
- You owe money   Spending
- You don't have enough money   Earning
- You don't have a money magnet   Transfers

Once a problem is correctly categorized according to the Nine Words of Generic Human Studies it will be much easier to

Chapter 21: The Nine Words of Generic Human Studies

solve. There's a very good chance your problem is a "generic problem" and thus will have a "generic solution."

A generic problem means that this problem has already occurred so many times to average people in the past that there is already a known solution. Just apply the generic solution that solves this known problem. If there is more than one generic solution, pick the one you like best. If that doesn't work, try the next one, etc.

If your problem is not a generic problem, put it aside for a while and clean up some more of your generic problems. The idea here is maybe you are being bitten by 20 snakes. See if you can quickly cut the number of snakes biting you down to six or seven. The more snakes not biting you the better. Once you've cleared up most of the generic problems, then go back to the non-generic problem and work on them if any of them are still there. There's a good chance they won't be.

GENERIC HUMAN STUDIES

The promise of GHS is that we all are human. Mentally speaking, you can't know everything you need to know before you take on the study of Generic Human Studies.

However, it turns out that mankind has already accumulated a massive amount of knowledge for solving problems that is true, right and lasting. If we look to solutions that have already been consolidated and quantified for the majority of generic problems that occur, without making up new terms or pretending we invented it, we already know how to solve at least 80% of the problems facing most individuals.

Answers to the majority of human problems were discovered long ago. Instead of sharing and teaching this knowledge in simple terms, it appears that certain people want to pretend they invented something new and give it a fancy name, so they can charge a lot of money for it. This keeps anything new they might have contributed from becoming a common knowledge.

Even worse, common knowledge is often repackaged as something new and sold for high prices, again by people just trying to make money. This only turns people off once they realize they are being duped by rehashed ideas under a different name.

GHS was established in 1986 at which time it consolidated a massive amount of information from a multitude of sources prior to this time. The specific details are recorded in the book, **What is Generic Human Studies?**

As I write this now in 2020, I still haven't seen anything new come out since this time that wasn't already known. Every year the same information is being repackaged in some new way for some new reason like it didn't already exist.

If people would just learn what we already know, most people would be able to solve their everyday life problems and move on to create and enjoy their happy lives.

For the readers of this book, you have been introduced to the GHS nomenclature, so you can understand how to evaluate your specific human problems and seek solutions that are most probably already available.

Because you are a SELF-Parenting Practitioner you have the added bonus of understanding your Inner Parent and Inner Child and being able to communicate between the two. With the tools and understanding provided to you in this book, along with a few years/decades of daily SELF-Parenting practice and

Chapter 21: The Nine Words of Generic Human Studies

some concentrated effort, there's no situation or problem that is unsolvable by you.

Make a point of reading this volume at least once per year. As your SELF-Parenting awareness grows, so will you see more value within these pages to enable you to live your best life and share your experience with others.

All my best to you,

John K. Pollard, III

About the Author

John K. Pollard, III received his Chiropractic degree from Los Angeles College of Chiropractic (LACC) in 1976, graduating with distinction.

Subsequently he established and operated one of Southern California's original and most comprehensive wellness and natural therapy clinics, Family Chiropractic Center in Canoga Park, CA.

In 1987, he published *SELF-PARENTING: The Complete Guide to Your Inner Conversations*, creating the principles and practice of consciously parenting your Inner Child as an Inner Parent.

During this period, he was the featured guest of many radio, news, and television interviews, including CNN. As an author and thought leader his book was endorsed and recommended by respected and prominent psychological teachers such as Louise Hay, John Bradshaw, and Ken Keyes, Jr.

www.ingramcontent.com/pod-product-compliance
Lightning Source LLC
Chambersburg PA
CBHW050630300426
44112CB00012B/1730